Praise for *Unfit to Fight*

"Amber Smith has written 'the' book on woke policies in the military and what it means to readiness. *Unfit to Fight* is a must-read by anyone interested in understanding what woke policies have done to our military and how to fix it. Amber has 'been there,' from fighting in combat to fighting the bureaucratic wars in the Pentagon. I love this book. It is a fast read, and her words come from the heart. She knows from experience what befalls a military whose leadership has forgotten its primary mission of deterrence and if it fails, to fight and win our nation's wars. I want Amber on my side as we try to restore the military to protect our nation. Well done, Amber!"

> —LTG (Ret.) Keith Kellogg, US Army, former National Security Advisor to Vice-President Mike Pence and chief of staff of the National Security Council.

"Amber absolutely nails it with *Unfit to Fight*. She exposes the terrifying truth of the downward spiral of our current military and how its loss of mission focus puts our country in grave danger. It's a must-read for anyone who cares about our nation's future and their family's safety and security."

> —Buck Sexton, co-host of *The Clay Travis & Buck Sexton Show* and former CIA officer

"Absolutely fantastic. Amber knocks it out of the park with *Unfit to Fight*. She reveals how politicized Pentagon leadership has jeopardized our national security by prioritizing ideological agendas over winning wars. This book is a wake-up call for every American on the risks we currently face with a weak, woke military. If you are concerned about the future and value the security of our nation, read this book. Don't miss it!"

> —Jesse Kelly, Host of the Jesse Kelly Show & 'I'm Right' and author of *The Anti-Communist Manifesto*

"Amber speaks to one of the most pressing issues of our time: a military in decline. What was once the fiercest fighting force in the world has been reduced by our leaders to drag queen videos, pronouns, and wokeness. The only way to solve a problem is to get to the root cause and expose the rot from within. Amber, who has bravely served our country, shines a light on what's plaguing our military in *Unfit to Fight*."

 —**Lisa Boothe,** host of *The Truth with Lisa Boothe*

"Wokism in the military is an existential threat to the United States and a betrayal of the American ethos 'E Pluribus Unum.' In an increasingly dangerous world, when unselfish leadership and a strong military are needed more than ever to prevent major wars, Amber Smith is a patriot sounding the alarm before it's too late. *Unfit to Fight* is a must-read for everyone who loves the military, which means accepting hard truths and the essential need for immediate course correction."

 —**Katie Pavlich,** Fox News contributor and *New York Times* bestselling author

UNFIT TO FIGHT
How Woke Policies Are
Destroying Our Military

AMBER SMITH

Since 1947
REGNERY
An Imprint of Skyhorse Publishing, Inc.

Regnery books may be purchased in bulk at special discounts for sales
promotion, corporate gifts, fund-raising, or educational purposes. Special
editions can also be created to specifications. For details, contact the Special
Sales Department, Regnery, 307 West 36th Street, 11th Floor, New York,
NY 10018 or info@skyhorsepublishing.com.

Regnery® is a registered trademark and its colophon is a trademark of
Skyhorse Publishing Inc.®, a Delaware corporation.

Visit our website at www.regnery.com.
Please follow our publisher Tony Lyons on Instagram
@tonylyonsisuncertain.

10 9 8 7 6 5 4 3 2 1

Library of Congress Cataloging-in-Publication Data is available on file.

Cover design by John Caruso
Cover photograph by Shutterstock

Print ISBN: 978-1-68451-480-9
eBook ISBN: 978-1-68451-563-9

Printed in the United States of America

For my incredible husband, who has dedicated
much of his life to defending our nation.

"Hard times create strong men,
strong men create good times;
good times create weak men,
weak men create hard times."

G. Michael Hopf

Contents

INTRODUCTION

"He who dares not offend cannot be honest."
Thomas Paine

This book isn't about me or the military I served in. That military doesn't exist anymore. Instead, I hope to provide a wakeup call to the current politically motivated military whose leadership has gone astray. It's about what those in today's military must deal with. It's about the dangers around the corner and what our nation will look like if our military doesn't return to a war-fighting, kill-your-enemies, mission-first fighting force.

I love this country and everything she stands for and represents. So much so that I served for over seven and a half years as an OH-58D Kiowa Warrior pilot in command and air mission commander in the 101st Airborne Division and spent two years in the Middle East flying low-level missions in Iraq and Afghanistan. I took out enemy targets. The enemy tried to kill me more times than I could count. I had an AK-47 round stop about twelve inches behind my back while flying a mission in Iraq. I had friends and colleagues who were killed or wounded. I saw the lives destroyed. I saw the painful bureaucracy, leadership failures, and political pressure inflicted on those who have to enact the decisions made from fancy PowerPoint presentations presented in an air-conditioned office in D.C., thousands of miles away from the realities of combat.

I am proud of my service. I didn't join for political reasons. I joined because our nation was viciously attacked, and innocent, unsuspecting Americans were killed in the most brutal fashion on 9/11. Watching the towers fall lit a fire inside me, and I knew I wanted to help protect the nation I loved. I am forever proud and grateful to be within the exclusive brotherhood and sisterhood of those who raised their right hand and swore an oath to the Constitution to protect and defend this country. After 9/11, watching the nation unify and put our individual differences aside was an incredible thing to witness. It seemed as if all Americans had a shared interest not only in our nation's safety but in revenge as well. The Authorized Use of Military Force (AUMF), the war authorization for the Afghanistan war, only had one dissenting vote in Congress.[1] One. That is almost unimaginable in today's political climate.

I love the military and the time I served. It was hard. It was challenging. It straight up kicked my ass at times. It opened my eyes to the good, the bad, and the very ugly realities of the world. But it made me strong. It was rewarding. It gave me confidence in my abilities, decision-making, and character. I knew who I was and what I was capable of. It made me realize that no matter the hardship, the adversity, or the sorrow, I would persevere, regardless of the situation. That is what the military gave me: discipline, structure, and purpose. Unfortunately, I saw what some bad military leaders looked like. And fortunately, I saw what good leaders looked like.

But now, wokeism has infiltrated the military. "Woke" is the progressive liberal ideology aimed at destroying traditional norms in every aspect of our society and nation. Most people didn't assume the military was at risk for becoming woke like other vulnerable institutions, such as the public education system or the medical industry. After all, the military's biggest regions for recruitment are red states. People who want to serve are usually patriotic and believe in this country and her values, enough to die for it if needed. But woke ideology spares nothing. The military is no exception. Diversity, equity, inclusion, transgender policy, double standards, quotas, mismanaged wars, vaccine mandates, Critical Race Theory, woke policies, toxic leadership, failed leadership, failed promotion structure, failed pay incentives, and zero leadership accountability are killing morale at the tactical and operational level. It has contributed to the worst recruitment crisis since the end of the Vietnam War. A retention crisis is looming. The all-volunteer force is on the edge of collapse. Young Americans are paying attention; they see these problems and don't want to serve anymore. More and more service members aren't going the distance, trying to make a career out of the military, but rather they want to get out as soon as their contract is up.

Young soldiers trust their leaders. It's an innocent and almost blind trust to follow those who lead them. They count on them, rely on them to make the best decisions in combat, and believe in their competence and uprightness. That trust is vital to the health of the commander-subordinate relationship. And that relationship is vital to winning battles in combat. It's a relationship that shouldn't be taken for granted. Once that trust starts to dissipate, effectiveness breaks down. Men and women aren't going to fight for a leader they despise or that they know doesn't have their best interests at heart. That broken trust begins at the individual leader level, but expands to the institution when a soldier looks behind the curtain and sees the true nature of the woke, politically driven establishment the Department of Defense has become.

For the armed forces, there is one overriding question: Do the issues the military is focused on make for a stronger, more lethal fighting force capable of deterring and defeating our enemy? Everything else depends on the answer to this question. If the answer to any specific issue is no, then that issue is a distraction from the mission. And when a distraction takes away focus and training from the force, it puts our national security at risk.

Service members selflessly sign up to serve and protect our nation, sometimes with their lives. That's not something I take for granted, especially regarding those who do their best, day in and day out, despite the unnecessary challenges they face because of political and woke policies pushed down from above. Despite it all, when young Americans sign up to fight, they deserve the best leadership on this planet and an apolitical military institution. What they do not need is fickle leadership that follows the latest social trends. Or to serve and protect a country with a two-tiered military justice system. Or one that allows leaders to follow the rules when they feel like it yet punishes those who serve under them who might question their actions. Our service members deserve better than what they are getting from military leadership. Sadly, I hardly recognize the military in which I once served.

Years after my time in the Army, I had the honor of being appointed by the President of the United States to serve as the deputy assistant to the Secretary of Defense for Outreach in Public Affairs at the Pentagon. The juxtaposition of serving once at the tactical level, flying low-level combat missions, to working in the E-Ring at the Pentagon was incredible. I saw a political institution that was not only reluctant to change and innovate, but one that had internal political agendas of its own. It was not focused on strategy for winning the wars but strategies for how these wars were being perceived. I saw an organization that was nearly paralyzed by fear of its reputation in the media. The Pentagon operates like a firehouse that is constantly getting calls to respond to a fire. It is constant chaos. It bounces from one fire to the next. The focus is on putting out current fires instead of trying to prevent them in the future. Unfortunately, many of those fires are self-inflicted.

Men and women who wear the uniform and work at the tactical and operational level don't deserve this. They are the ones who don't get a say and don't have a voice, yet carry the weight, wounds, and grief caused by the policies they were ordered to enforce when there was no logic behind them. They often feel tossed aside by the government of the nation they love and signed up to defend.

This book exposes what is hiding in plain sight—toxic military leadership, which is no longer focused on protecting the force, accomplishing the mission, and winning wars, but is concerned with appeasing woke politicians in D.C. who have the next election to win. I take no pride in exposing the failures of the military that I love. I do so out of deep admiration and respect for those who choose to wear the uniform and deserve better than what they have been given after the sacrifices they have made.

We are at a crossroads in our nation right now. Our military is not a social experiment. It shouldn't follow political agendas that change every two to four years. Its generals and leaders should be solely focused on being able to lead a military that is so strong that it provides the strongest possible deterrence to our enemies. And in those times it isn't able to deter, it can use every bit of military might to swiftly and effectively destroy those enemies. Service members should be able to trust that their senior leaders have their best interest at heart and will do everything in their power to ensure that they come home from the conflicts and wars they are ordered to fight in. The harsh reality is that an all-volunteer military is not sustainable in its current condition. Things must change rapidly before it's too late. This change must be drastic.

If an enemy were looking to divide America, as we are seeing today, the best way would be to break down the trust and professionalism the American people have for decades taken for granted in our military.

Woke, poisonous policies are destroying the military from the inside out. No enemy nation's interference is needed. And it has happened faster than most could believe. China, Russia, Iran, North Korea, and more are watching and learning every day what our military is capable of, as well as what it is not capable of. Sadly, with the military's current state, it will not be able to fight and destroy our adversaries on multiple fronts. With World War III knocking at our door, the nation and our military are desperate for leadership to turn this ship around. Let's just hope World War III doesn't come first.

CHAPTER I

We Have a Problem

*"A great civilization is not conquered from without, until
it has destroyed itself from within."*

Ariel Durant

A nuclear World War III is now a realistic threat. Peer adversary China continues to threaten to invade Taiwan. Tensions surrounding the US proxy war with Russia in Ukraine are increasing daily. Iranian proxy forces and drones in Syria continue to attack American service members and allies. US foreign policy is in free fall around the world. The dollar is in a long decline.[1] Foreigners are dropping the dollar because they don't think it is reliable. The national debt is skyrocketing. But threats are not only from nation-states. Despite twenty years of war and trillions of dollars, terror groups remain a threat. In March 2023, the CENTCOM commander, General Michael Kurilla, briefed the Senate Arms Services Committee that in six months, ISIS-K—the Islamic States Afghanistan branch—will be able to strike Western allies and interests abroad with no warning.[2]

The threat of a hot war with both China and Russia is significant and perhaps imminent. The reality of this war would have dire consequences. The challenges our military would face are something military leadership and its forces haven't seen since World War II. The current state of the US military cannot effectively fight a two-front war against two peer adversaries in conjunction with every other task required of it. For too long, politicians, society, and the military have gotten used to fighting sandal-wearing goat herders with AK-47s in the Middle East. It gave many leaders an inflated ego and a false sense of security in our military capabilities. Not that it should have, because despite our technological superiority, ISIS was able to rage through Iraq in 2014, and the Taliban now rule Afghanistan.

A fight with Russia, China, or both will not be the same as fighting off terrorists in Afghanistan or Iraq. It will be naval warfare, waves of fighters landing on beaches under heavy machine gun fire and drone swarms and facing a modern and capable air force. Hundreds of thousands, if not millions, will die. It will be a war against two nuclear superpowers, with Russia having the world's largest stockpile of nuclear weapons. It will be a world war, a war to end all wars. With this threat, one would likely assume military leadership is focused on nothing other than training, readiness, and effectiveness. Wrong. The military is currently focused on activities that weaken it from the inside out with woke appeasement, distractions, and worries about individual feelings. What comes next is nothing short of terrifying, as it appears that the United States of America, for the first time in almost a century, is at risk of losing a major war.

Eighty years ago, young, tough, patriotic American men left their families behind and traveled halfway around the world to fight an enemy they had never seen, not knowing if they would ever see their loved ones again. They stormed the beaches at Normandy, scaled Point du Hac, and fought our enemy in horrid conditions throughout the Pacific. Why did they make that sacrifice? Because they believed that our great nation and our way of life were worth defending for future generations. Because America is that special, that unique, and that rare.

They were willing to give their all to preserve what they loved most: freedom. They knew freedom wasn't a handout or a nation without laws or accountability; it was the opportunity to pursue the American Dream. To work hard and be proud of their accomplishments. Military leaders were still held accountable for the wars they were charged with winning and were given the confidence and authority to fight them.

But over the decades since World War II, bureaucracy has allowed war and conflict to become a profitable business. The Pentagon has prioritized political agendas and has turned into an indoctrination institution. Our politicians and generals are addicted to conflict but not to winning; success in their professional careers depends on going to war and staying at war, regardless of battlefield success or lack thereof. War validates their existence. Their facility at keeping the war machine turning gives them the experience necessary to get their next job, either in uniform or on the board at a defense industry prime contractor. Worse, they are not held accountable for their mismanagement and loss.

Generals have become a revered class of citizens, which is ironic given the US military has not won a major war since World War II. Still, war has become a lucrative business. The military industrial complex is a revolving door for generals, admirals, and Pentagon officials. It is normal for generals and senior military leaders to lie while testifying under oath to Congress to avoid further scrutiny for their systemic failures. They have learned they won't face any consequences—even when it is something as serious as the status of a conflict in which young Americans are being sent to fight and die.

Americans have caught on; they see generals and politicians lie about the political reasons for going to war and no longer want to sign up to die. The military cannot meet its own recruitment numbers, and when they realized they couldn't, they lowered the goals. Double standards, hypocrisy, and lowering standards to serve the ill-defined goals of diversity, equity, and inclusion proved a disaster, but the leadership, contrary to all evidence, is spinning its failure as success. Generals and other senior military leaders get into public Twitter battles to put down members of the media they disagree with. And with adversarial nations looming as peer competitors, military officials shift focus and parrot political talking points on climate change and domestic extremism, touting them as the biggest threats to our national security.

While the military has been able to limp along for the last two decades hiding behind a never-ending defense budget brought on by the post-9/11 wars, we have started to see the consequences of a wandering focus, shifting from war fighting and accomplishing the mission to progressive political and activist ideology. Morale is in the tank. Seasoned warfighters are turning down commands and promotions in order to fast-track their departure from the military. The new military values equity over equality. The military now prioritizes wokeness over readiness.

Let me assure you that the US military is an unrecognizable force from even a decade ago. The military has undergone drastic and rapid reforms over the last decade—and not for the better. There's one common denominator: lost mission focus. There's no accountability, nor even minimal oversight from Congress. There's toxic leadership and fiscal irresponsibility. The military has lost its sense of self, its purpose. Its spokesmen deny this and talk of "warfighting" and readiness whenever its antics are questioned. But such talk is in vain when it does not walk the walk. Woke ideology has taken over the Department of Defense, and like a cancer it has rapidly spread throughout the institution, damaging everything in its wake. Some policies are forced on the Department of Defense as executive orders from the President of the United States. Some are not. Regardless, the Pentagon is responsible for any plans they create, the orders they give, and the policies they enforce within the branches. They own their failures.

Much of military leadership refuses to even acknowledge wokeism's effects on the force. The Army Secretary said she doesn't know what woke means. Secretary of Defense Lloyd Austin said he doesn't get what the issue with Critical Race Theory (CRT) is—and that the Department of Defense (DOD) doesn't teach it anyway (which is false). Others openly embrace it. General Milley, the recently retired chairman of the Joint Chiefs of Staff, said he thinks Critical Race Theory in military education is essential. Whether denied or accepted, CRT, gender ideology, and social justice are taking priority over mission focus and military readiness. All of this is a distraction from allowing those who patriotically wear the uniform to accomplish the mission. Service members are told they are the problem, that they are racists, sexists, and even extremists. The military has kicked out battle-trained, proven combat veterans with years of experience owing to their refusal to take the COVID vaccine. The military is spending tax dollars on recruiting ads that appeal to LGBTQ+ constituencies. It's ordering "stand down days" after national political events, lowering standards to ensure the retention of a set number of women, and even allowing drag queen shows on military bases.

The military's focus is no longer on winning wars and destroying our enemies—it is an indoctrination institution that pushes pronouns, identity politics, and DEI propaganda over accomplishing the mission. Many in leadership positions say that "the military should reflect society" or "the military should look like America" in an attempt to justify this woke agenda. But that's a delusion. The military should not be focused on trying to be a mirror image of society. That contributes nothing to a force whose sole purpose should be accomplishing the mission. The military should be composed of young Americans who want to serve—in the patriotic sense of destroying our enemies with violence to win wars and protect our way of life.[3]

This is not a reflection of those who serve or who joined as their patriotic duty to protect our nation from those who wish us harm. Rather, it is a harsh indictment of Pentagon leadership and the generals who enforce propaganda and political agendas over winning wars, which has contributed to a historic recruitment crisis.[4] The already small percentage of Americans who are eligible to serve don't want to. In 2022, the Army missed its recruitment goal by 25 percent. That means the Army failed to add fifteen thousand new soldiers, significantly missing its own mark and putting the decline of a once healthy Army on full display.[5]

In July 2022, Army leadership knew the announcement of its failed recruitment numbers would send shockwaves through defense stakeholders and defense media. The Army tried to mitigate the panic by writing a memo from the secretary of the Army, Christine Wormuth, and the chief of staff of the Army, General McConnville, to address these failures.[6] But really, the memo was more of an attempt to curtail a PR disaster than any sort of solution to the Army's problem. The memo failed to address the elephant in the room: self-inflicted leadership problems, woke ideologies, the disastrous withdrawal from Afghanistan, lack of trust and confidence, and parents not recommending service to their children because of all of the above. The memo was written to assure commanders and service members that the recruiting crisis wasn't a crisis, just a blip on the radar that they'd attempt to fix by throwing money at the problem for short term gains. The memo did not address any internal contributing factors or how to address them. In the summer of 2022, the Army began extending fifty-thousand-dollar signing bonuses to those soon-to-be soldiers who qualified.[7]

The Air Force Academy has created a new program called the American Oath Project, led by students and one faculty member, to try to educate fellow students on the meaning of the oath of office after many cadets complained that they couldn't actually articulate what the oath meant and how it applied to upholding the Constitution. Many cadets struggled with the "why."[8] If they don't understand the meaning of the oath they swore to defend, how will they stay motivated to defend it? While the project itself seems necessary, it reveals a broader issue. Many feel the military has not focused on educating its young leaders on the importance of constitutional principles and civil-military relations, the reason behind a civilian-controlled military, and why that military should be apolitical. The academy does have a core civics class for sophomores titled "Introduction to American Government and National Security." Still, the entire course only has five lessons on the Constitution and civ-mil relations.[9] If the cadets at a service academy don't understand the Constitution's role in the military and the military's role in defending it, how can the rest of American society be expected to?

This is a harbinger of a society in decline. America's youth are not being taught the foundation of our nation, including civics, constitutional literacy, patriotic history, or what makes this nation great and worth preserving. CRT teaches them the opposite—substituting a perceived negative, oppressive, and shameful past. No one should be surprised that cadets aren't exactly sure what it is they are there to uphold. It is sad and terrifying for our nation, but perhaps understandable given how divided our country is and taking into account elite obsession with woke ideology. Trying to counter this agenda in college is sadly too late.

How could things have changed so rapidly from the Greatest Generation to an Absent Generation? Sadly, much of the damage is self-inflicted. The fundamental shift in military culture began after President Obama took office in 2008. Eight years proved enough time to instigate generational changes that run quite deep. While President Trump attempted to reverse much of the politicization at the Pentagon, President Biden quickly overturned these orders once he took office.

We live in a culture that has allowed the civilian population to become disconnected from those tasked with defending the freedoms and liberties we enjoy. An attitude of apathy and disregard for military operations and conflicts has metastasized to large sectors of the culture. In conjunction with political and military leadership, this disconnect has led the Department of Defense to evolve into an institution focused on pronouns and identity politics to appease a segment of the population that could not care less about the military or its mission. The Pentagon has become a political institution prioritizing progressive culture, diversity, equity, and inclusion. These policies that ebb and flow with presidential administrations are destructive to our military—they have real and long-term consequences to recruitment, retention, and readiness, which we are already seeing today. Potential recruits, the ones that are fit enough and smart enough to serve, realize that they are being used as political pawns. The service members that make up our nation's military are now held hostage to gender quotas, pronouns, transgender appeasement, COVID vaccine mandates, DEI, extremisms training, extremist stand-down days, and more.[10]

Service members used to trust their leaders, both political and military. They used to believe in the national ideals they were fighting for. But with the chaotic and failed withdrawal from Afghanistan, and with transgender women (biological men) being allowed to share showers and bathrooms with women, service members are starting to ask: What is my service for? Why am I making the sacrifices that come with military service such as long and consistent deployments, moving every couple of years, being away from family, and missing out on birthdays, graduations, weddings, and anniversaries?

Quality of life has also declined. The defense budget is nearly $842 billion for the fiscal year 2024.[11] Despite that massive number, the DOD is still making service members live in mold-infested barracks and hazardous conditions in on-post family housing, despite the constant reassurance that officials will fix the problem.[12] Other military families have faced water leaks, rotten wood, raw sewage, and even "poop falling from the ceiling."[13] Signing up to serve your country shouldn't mean you accept substandard living conditions that threaten you and your family's health. Our service members deserve better than this.

The number of Americans who have held the military institution in high regard and trust over the last few decades has declined rapidly. In 2018, 70 percent of Americans had a great deal of trust and confidence in the military. In 2021, that dropped to 56 percent. In 2022, it had fallen to 48 percent. That's an alarming downward trend in such a short amount of time. The same 2022 poll found that 62 percent of Americans think military leadership is overly politicized, while 50 percent believe the military's wokeness is damaging effectiveness.[14]

It's even worse for active duty military. Trust and confidence are rapidly eroding within the military, directly related to woke policies. A 2022 Maru/Blue poll for the Heritage Foundation think tank asked, "To what degree have the following events or reports decreased your trust in the military?" Seventy-one percent said the withdrawal from Afghanistan; 64 percent said the fact that the military is pursuing all-electric vehicles; 65 percent said the military being required to pay for travel for service members' abortions; 69 percent said CRT being on the Chief of Naval Operations reading list; 70 percent said reduction in physical fitness standards to "even the playing field"; 70 percent said focusing on climate change as a national security threat. And coming in as the top reason for service members losing trust in the military, at 80 percent: allowing unrestricted service to transgenders. These are absolutely damning numbers.[15]

The Pentagon now considers climate change a legitimate national security issue. Since the early days of the Obama administration, the Pentagon has recognized climate change as a threat and its potential to affect where and how the military operates around the globe. Labeling this supposed danger as a priority and urgency has only increased since then. The Pentagon has significantly increased its resources, narrative, and posture to combat climate change.[16] During the Trump administration, the National Defense Strategy did not focus on climate change nor treat it as a priority.[17] That quickly changed when Biden took office.

Within the first week of his presidency, on January 27, 2021, President Biden signed executive order 14008, Tackling Climate Crisis at Home and Abroad.[18] It required all federal agencies to make climate change their number one priority. The DOD, sensing funding opportunities for new bureaucratic power structures, immediately jumped to prioritize incorporating "green" wargaming, and made climate change mitigation a part of the national defense strategy with other policy directives.[19]

"The Department will immediately take appropriate policy actions to prioritize climate change considerations in our activities and risk assessments to mitigate this driver of insecurity," Secretary Austin said. It will be accomplished by "including the security implications of climate change in our risk analyses, strategy development, and planning guidance."[20]

In other words, we intend to waste everyone's time and, in doing so, weaken the force. A vague priority such as this takes away war fighting resources and diffuses personnel's focus on the mission. If climate change is that important to the Biden administration, they can set up a separate White House interagency task force to tackle it. Forcing the DOD to prioritize the nebulous climate threat and incorporating such considerations into all aspects of daily operations detracts from the real, imminent threats our nation faces every day, like Russia and China.

In early January 2023, President Joe Biden told an audience at a fundraiser that climate change was the biggest threat to humanity, even more significant than nuclear war: "If we don't stay under 1.5 degrees Celsius, we're going to have a real problem. It's the single-most existential threat to humanity we've ever faced, including nuclear weapons," Biden said.[21] General Milley later agreed with President Biden but added that China and Russia might also be something of a threat in a military context.[22]

Climate change is not a menace to our national security. It is a scare tactic by lobbyists to push a green agenda and a trillion-dollar government subsidized industry. The Chinese military is what a threat actually looks like. Service members who are deployed worldwide see real threats with their own eyes: the Taliban in Afghanistan, the war in Ukraine, China's aggression in the South China Sea, and attacks by Iranian-made drones in Syria. That breeds a discord and distrust between the warfighter and leadership. The ones who have to fight in the real world and face its consequences are living in a different, harsher reality than the ones who merely talk about military priorities in Washington, D.C.

China has a long-term strategy to surpass the United States and become the dominant global power. They are looking down the road fifty, even a hundred years. Meanwhile, the US military is on a four-year political cycle that follows political winds and what's trending on social media.[23] American generals are more focused on scheduling book interviews to bash former presidents and media appearances to burnish their images than solving looming problems like recruitment and retention issues and focusing on preparing our fighting force for the next war.

Pentagon and military leadership need to self-reflect and acknowledge that they must reverse course. Firing generals for lack of performance should make a comeback. Accountability is the way forward. The top military brass needs to stop looking outward and making excuses. It's time to look inward to bring about beneficial changes. The DOD should operate like a war-fighting institution rather than a D.C. political bureaucracy.

Congress must perform its constitutional duty and provide proper oversight of military actions, conflicts, and wars. Congress commands the purse strings. It's time to exert control over the matter and start using this power. One quick way to start: stop blanket NDAA funding that provides almost no oversight to conflicts the DOD is involved in. And since Joe Biden won't do it, Congress must hold generals and political leaders accountable for the Pentagon's failures. Stop allowing the Pentagon to "investigate" itself and clear itself of all wrongdoing. This practice has become an embarrassment.

The deteriorated trust in Pentagon leadership by the civilian population and those who serve puts the United States at extreme risk of losing a future war. Such a loss would mean a drastic and devastating change in the American way of life. This is the real danger of a woke military whose policies are poisoning the institution from the inside out, causing crises of recruitment, retention, morale, and, most important, readiness. The military has gotten too political and too distracted, and the bureaucracy has gotten too big. It can't innovate. Red tape abounds. It can't get its soldiers the most up-to-date equipment with the latest technology. The military must get back to basics. It needs to return to being the merit-based institution that has worked for generations. And with Russia and China at our doorstep, there is no more time for victimhood.

So the Pentagon is in a nosedive. Without self-reflection and correction, it will crash and burn. The military must stop chasing social trends to appease demographics in an attempt to make the institution a more likable brand. The military must return to its roots, return to a meritocracy, reject social agendas, avoid politicization, stick to standards, and promote a culture that values innovation and accepts risk. Leaders must be held accountable for losing wars. The military thrives when it is a mission-first organization. In fact, it can't operate effectively any other way.

Here's a pretty simple litmus test: Is the policy a distraction that takes away from focusing on mission capabilities and readiness, or does it strengthen the force and enhance mission capabilities and readiness?

The military must get out of the appeasement business. Wearing the US military uniform is not a right or guarantee. Not everyone is qualified or should be allowed to serve.

The danger of this crisis is difficult to overstate. Without our military, we don't have a country. Part of having a strong nation, a free nation, and one that is the dominant world power is having a strong military that leverages its potential power and might in the form of deterrence. One that makes our adversaries think twice about unprovoked aggression. When our adversaries are not continually worried about finding themselves the focus of the wrath of the US military, we're in a perilous place. And if that happens long enough, freedom will no longer ring.

CHAPTER 2

Make Generals Great Again

"If a private loses a rifle, he gets charged with a crime. If a general loses a war, he gets promoted."

Lieutenant Colonel Paul Yingling

A drastic shift in leadership accountability crept in following World War II: generals stopped getting fired for poor performance. It is not a coincidence that since then we have not won a single significant war. To this day, it is rare for a general to be fired, regardless of the significance of his failures on the battlefield. In World War II and prior, civilian oversight or military command would commonly get rid of generals. While they may have been good officers until that point, if they couldn't lead, they got fired and were replaced with men who could. This is fairly brutal logic that works when the stakes are as high as they are in war. A general could either do the job, succeed, and prove his leadership abilities in a short amount of time, or if not, be fired. There was no waiting around. There wasn't even much drama to it. And it worked. It incentivized officers to excel, work hard, and have tangible wins.[1]

But something else changed. By Vietnam, the Department of Defense's internal culture had become stagnant, bureaucratic, and risk-averse. Despite their poor performance, military commanders getting fired just didn't have a good ring to it in the headlines across the country. Regardless of the individual circumstances surrounding a given firing, it raised internal concerns about the military's public perception—it made the entire organization look incompetent.[2] At least that was the thought. But a Department of Defense that rarely holds top leadership accountable has produced terrible consequences. Generals have become conformists, yes-men, and have kept their heads down to stay out of the negative spotlight. Not only that, but there is no punishment for losing and, therefore, no incentive for a general to actually work hard to make good, strategic decisions. It's no longer about the men they lead; it's about their career and climbing. Success is marked at retirement by a board seat for a prime defense contractor. Today's generals often view the biggest enemy as a hearing on Capitol Hill where they are required to begrudgingly answer congressmen's questions, or a cable news host who calls them out on their antics. Worse yet, generals simply aren't worried about being inept. There is no punishment for it. All a general has to do is toe the party line, outlast others, and he will continue to take his absurdly high paycheck and benefits and eventually be able to accept the offerings of undeserving board seats after retirement. With generals like these, it's no wonder we haven't been able to win the post-9/11 wars.

It should come as no surprise that a general such as Lloyd Austin, with massive failures occurring under his commands during the Obama administration, finds himself as Secretary of Defense in the Biden administration. President Biden nominated retired four-star general Lloyd Austin as the first Black secretary of defense,[3] saying he wanted a presidential cabinet that looks like America.[4] Prior to being selected to serve as the twenty-eighth secretary of defense, Austin meandered through the ranks of the US Army and, after forty-one years, retired as a four-star general.[5] General Austin faced his share of scandal and controversy throughout his career, especially in the years following stars on his shoulders.

In 2012, General Austin was nominated by President Obama to command Central Command, known as CENTCOM, and confirmed in March 2013.[6] He was preceded by General James Mattis. CENTCOM is responsible for an area of operation that spans twenty nations, including Iraq, Syria, Afghanistan, Egypt, Iran, Israel, and most of the Middle East. As part of his duties, General Austin was in charge of the fight against the terrorist group ISIS, which established a caliphate holding territory throughout Iraq and Syria and horrified the world with some of the most heinous actions seen since the Dark Ages. He was tactically and operationally in charge of the area when ISIS captured hundreds of US military tanks, vehicles, and other equipment and paraded them around for the world to see.[7] In a September 2015 testimony in front of Congress, General Austin admitted that the military program that was supposed to instruct and equip moderate Syrian rebels and provide 5,400 fighters in the first year had, six months into the program and after a cost to CENTCOM of $42 million, only trained fifty-four fighters. When Austin was questioned in Congress about how many of those fifty-four had actually remained active, he replied, "It's a small number," before revealing that the small number was four to five people.[8] That's not a typo: Austin's CENTCOM spent $42 million US tax dollars to train four to five Syrian rebels. For those who served under his leadership in CENTCOM's area of operation, his reputation for indecisiveness was an open secret.

Aside from the failures in Iraq and Syria under Austin's leadership, another major scandal was brewing. In 2014, under General Austin's command, CENTCOM began distorting intelligence to manipulate policy in Washington, D.C. Intelligence assessments that were critical of the status and capabilities of the US-trained Iraqi security forces were intentionally skewed and delayed to paint a more favorable picture of the situation in the fight against ISIS. Words describing the Iraqi military, such as "'slow,' 'stalled,' and 'retreat' were changed to 'deliberate' and 'relocated.'"[9] Any US soldier on the battlefield knew the truth, especially any charged with the direct training of those Iraqi forces.

If that wasn't bad enough, in 2015 the CENTCOM director of intelligence, General Steven Grove, reportedly blocked negative intel on the Iraqi Security Forces from making it to the President's Daily Briefing for President Obama—a top secret daily intel assessment of global events—in order for his boss, General Austin, to first brief Congress about the United States fighting against ISIS. General Grove took it upon himself to prevent essential information from moving up the chain in order to paint a more favorable picture of CENTCOM, just in time for Austin to request more funding from Congress. Both the Defense Intelligence Agency and CENTCOM intel analysts agreed in their assessment that Iraqi security forces would not be able to retake Mosul from ISIS by the end of 2015.[10] But Grove halted the intel assessment from moving through its channels by forcing intelligence reassessments until Austin had testified in front of Congress that the campaign against ISIS was going well.[11] This is like a weatherman who works for a beach resort changing the forecast from rain to sunshine so that vacationers book more rooms at the hotel.

The testimony was a contradiction of known facts. General Austin testified that "ISIL [the military's term for ISIS] is losing this fight" and that "we're about where we said that we would be in the execution of our military campaign plan," emphasizing that ISIS was on the run and the military's "train and equip" strategy was working as planned, but that the Pentagon still needed $715 million more dollars to see it through. Just another three-quarters of a billion dollars, and success was on the way.[12] Of course, many generals have said something to Congress to the effect of, "I just need a little more, and I can win this war. . . ." But most are not testifying when a situation exactly opposite to the picture they paint is already known to be developing.

A little over six months later, Austin testified before Congress again, and this time completely contradicted the chairman of the Joint Chiefs of Staff, General Demsey, who the week prior, in front of Congress, stated that US Forces were in a "tactical stalemate" with ISIS. After hearing the rose-colored, misrepresentative, and downright misleading report from the CENTCOM Commander, Senator John McCain did not hold back on General Austin: "I have never heard testimony like this. . . . Never." He went on to say that in his thirty years serving on the committee, "I have never seen a hearing that is as divorced from the reality of every outside expert and what you are saying."[13] Once again, General Austin, the commander of the most strategically important area of operations in the world at the time, who was the recipient of the highest amount of military resources of any other combatant command, and who had the highest prioritization for additional resources and military power, appeared entirely incompetent.

Soon after, two separate federal investigations were underway to address allegations of intelligence manipulation out of CENTCOM. Congressional House Republicans launched a joint task force investigation made up of the House Intelligence Committee, the House Armed Services Committee, and the House Defense Appropriations Committee to get to the bottom of many accusations from intel officials that their intelligence was being altered to paint a rosy picture of the military's progress in the fight against ISIS. The Pentagon's inspector general launched an additional investigation after two intel analysts filed a written complaint claiming that their intel assessments had been downplayed or changed to match the public narrative that the fight against ISIS was going well. This included some intel briefed to the President of the United States. Fifty more analysts followed with the same complaint.[14]

The House joint task force investigation concluded that CENTCOM intelligence *was* manipulated, that significant evidence led to this conclusion. In addition to classified intelligence assessments being altered, the joint task force found that CENTCOM's knowledge of the situation was far from the rosy picture it had painted in public testimony and statements about the status of the fight against ISIS in Iraq and Syria, including General Austin's testimony to Congress.[15]

In stark contrast, the Pentagon's inspector general's investigation concluded, "We did not substantiate the most serious allegation, which was that intelligence was falsified."[16] The IG did note that there was "widespread perception of distortion"[17] surrounding CENTCOM intelligence, a significant lack of trust in intelligence leadership, a harsh work environment, and a failure of leadership to discuss the rationale behind decision-making. Fifty-two intel analysts do the right thing and speak truth to power, they all make the same accusation about intel manipulation, and the Pentagon's IG investigation chalks it up to leadership not communicating correctly with its subordinates? At best, Austin's command and leadership style is substandard; at worst, it signals a breach of honor and a political ploy. Unless these fifty-two intel analysts were all conspiring to speak out against their CENTCOM leaders, it seems that the CENTCOM leadership chose politics over truth. All of this could have been highlighted, leaders could have been held accountable, and future leaders tempted to play funding politics would have taken heed. But none of that happened. Perhaps the Pentagon should stop investigating itself since it never finds anything wrong with what is being investigated.

Politicized intelligence is dangerous when officials pick and choose information here and there to fit or create a particular narrative that drives a political agenda. Truth can go out the window. Unfortunately, this is nothing new. The CENTCOM intelligence manipulation accusation mirrors the handling of the 2002 and 2003 Iraq intelligence on the search for weapons of mass destruction.[18] Intel analysts must feel confident that their honest and truthful assessment matters. Intel assessments should not be altered to sway or influence a decision-maker—they should give the decision-maker the most accurate and unbiased information to make the best decision with the information available.

In 2016, Austin retired from CENTCOM and gave this statement regarding the politicized intelligence investigations:

> As a senior military commander, I always made it very clear that I expected transparent and unvarnished intelligence assessments. Those assessments represent one important aspect of what are a number of factors used by leadership to understand the situation on the ground and make appropriate decisions regarding operations and application of available resources. I did not in this instance, specific to the capability of the Iraqi Security Forces in 2015, nor any other instance direct any member of the CENTCOM staff to adjust intelligence products or delay their delivery, nor would I have tolerated such actions.[19]

Since this *was* done, it would appear that Austin was either a puppet that was easily manipulated by his staff or else he was complicit. Either way, he should have been relieved of command for his inability to manage his troops. And the failures and scandals didn't stop when Austin hung up his uniform. Instead, five years later he became the Secretary of Defense for the United States of America. What followed could be considered two of the worst decisions in recent military history.

As the Secretary of Defense, Secretary Austin was overall in charge of the 2021 Afghanistan withdrawal after President Biden capriciously announced the twenty-year war was over. The following withdrawal and evacuation was a failure of epic proportions. It was the biggest foreign policy disaster since the fall of Saigon at the end of the Vietnam War and was fraught with eerily similar images of embassy evacuations and desperate citizens clinging to American aircraft. It exposed our weaknesses, limitations, and double standards to our adversaries and allies. Our adversaries also got a significant glimpse into the US military and foreign policy decision-making process, or lack thereof. But worst of all, thirteen US service members and 170 Afghans were killed on August 26, 2021, when an ISIS-K suicide bomber blew himself up outside of Abby Gate at Kabul International Airport during the evacuation.[20] In the aftermath of the bombing, the United States conducted a rushed and retaliatory drone strike which ended up striking an innocent target. Ten innocent civilians were killed, seven of whom were children. For weeks the Pentagon maintained the strike was "righteous."[21] To this day, no one has been held accountable for this failure of epic proportions.

That same month, in August 2021, Secretary Austin announced the COVID vaccine mandate was in effect for the military to preserve the health and readiness of the force.[22] In fact, it did the opposite. The military shifted its posture to a 100 percent–vaccination agenda in a near-totalitarian manner. Religious, medical, and administrative exemptions were treated as a waste of commanders' time, and very few were approved. Specifically for religious exemptions, an inspector general investigation found that the military was not following the law that required each packet to receive individual review. Instead, blanket form letters were sent out to service members who had spent weeks creating their packets, conducting interviews, and ensuring they had all their documentation in order and all required forms filled entirely to military standards. The COVID vaccine mandate has done more to damage the force than service members contracting COVID ever has. On a morale level, it caused a rapid deterioration of trust between leaders and subordinates. And even for those who ended up taking the vaccine voluntarily, many felt coerced due to the threat of losing their jobs. Eight thousand four hundred skillful service members, many with priceless combat and leadership experience, were forced out of service.[23] With minimal notice, many had to leave behind medical benefits, pensions, and careers they loved. Many other service members were in limbo for over a year and a half, uncertain of their fate. After the vaccine mandate was forced to be revoked in the 2023 defense bill, the Pentagon continued to pursue punishment for those service members who refused to take the shot. All of this was brought about by orders issued by Secretary Lloyd Austin. These orders and policies could be enacted or reversed with his pen stroke. Austin's legacy of political theater seems to have followed him from his time as an indecisive commander at CENTCOM.

A year and a half after the monumental and tragic failure of the withdrawal from Afghanistan, Austin found himself once again back on Capitol Hill facing questions about his decision-making. At a House Armed Services Committee hearing, Congressman Jim Banks, an Afghanistan war veteran, asked Austin if he had any regrets about the Afghanistan withdrawal.

The defense secretary responded, "I support [President Biden's] decision. I don't have any regrets."[24]

Clearly Lloyd's answer went beyond policy and obedience to orders. It demonstrated a severe lack of empathy to the troops who fought in Afghanistan and the families of those who were killed.

"Mr. Austin, that is very telling," Congressman Banks said. He went on to ask if Austin had any specific regrets about how the withdrawal was handled, including the suicide bombing that killed thirteen US troops and 170 Afghan civilians. Austin continued, "I don't have any regrets."[25] It is sickening to think that the senior official in charge of our nation's military has zero regrets when asked about our nation's worst operational failure since Vietnam. He has zero regrets about the thirteen service members murdered at Abby Gate. He has zero regrets about the thousands of service members that lost their lives throughout the twenty-year war in Afghanistan. He has zero regrets about the tens of thousands of service members that lost limbs or suffer post-traumatic stress from countless deployments to war zones in Afghanistan. He has zero regrets about the Americans left behind. He has zero regrets about showing the world that the United States will leave our partners and allies that we have fought alongside at the drop of a hat if it is no longer politically convenient to continue fighting with them. He has zero regrets about overseeing operational failure after failure to complete a retrograde out of theater. Zero regrets.

Austin isn't the only senior-level Pentagon leader whose leadership abilities have proven inept. General Mark Milley found himself under fire in September 2021 after admitting he was interviewed for Watergate journalist Bob Woodward for his book, *Peril*. He also admitted to being interviewed by two other authors for separate books.[26] Perhaps General Milley might better serve the Constitution, the American people, and the President of the United States if he focused a little less on the media and a little more on doing his job. Sadly, that has become the main purpose of many senior military leadership positions: a chance for publicity in order to elevate one's chances in the private sector after retirement.

In Woodward and Costa's *Peril*, Milley admits to taking steps to prevent President Trump from ordering movement of nuclear weapons or launching a military strike. In 2020 and 2021 respectively, Mark Milley made two phone calls to his Chinese counterpart, General Li Zuocheng of the People's Liberation Army. First, on October 30, 2020, Milley called General Zuocheng after reading intelligence that said China believed America was preparing an attack on China. The *Washington Post* reported that General Milley said, "General Li, you and I have known each other for now five years. . . . If we're going to attack, I'm going to call you ahead of time. It's not going to be a surprise."[27] A few months later, after January 6, Speaker of the House Nancy Pelosi and General Milley spoke over the phone concerning ways to serve as a stopgap between the commander in chief and the military if Milley felt the president threatened world peace. Woodward and Costa also report that Speaker Nancy Pelosi discussed options with Milley to rein in the president's ability to perform his constitutionally defined duties if she or Miley found such actions "crazy" and not to their liking. Many hold these actions were tantamount to discussing a coup. According to the *Washington Post*, Pelosi asked, "What precautions are available to prevent an unstable president from initiating military hostilities or accessing the launch codes and ordering a nuclear strike?"[28] Milley went on to agree with her on the danger.[29] On January 8, Milley's second call to Chinese general Li Zuocheng occurred. Milley said, "We are 100 percent steady. Everything's fine. But democracy can be sloppy sometimes."[30] Later, Milley took it a step further. He personally called the Indo-Pacific commander and recommended pausing military exercises.[31]

At a Senate Arms Services Committee hearing in September 2021, Milley admitted President Trump wasn't planning to attack China. Senator Dan Sullivan asked Milley if he thought the Chinese would call Milley and give him a heads-up if that nation were to attack Taiwan. Milley answered no and then doubled down. He tried to reiterate that it was his job to de-escalate under all conditions.[32]

On the contrary. As the chairman of the Joint Chiefs of Staff, General Milley's primary responsibility was to provide the best military advice to the Commander in Chief.[33] The position carries no command authority. The chairman's role is not to de-escalate, it also very markedly is not to conspire with the speaker of the House on the early makings of a coup, and it surely is not to provide sensitive information about our nation's military plans to our most serious and dangerous adversary.

When President Trump left office, General Milley worked hard on rebranding his image. He felt his time serving under Trump had damaged his reputation, especially after posing for a photo in front of a burned-out church across the street from the White House after protestors had been cleared from the area. After that, it was obvious he wished to distance himself from Trump. Soon after, he realized that countering Trump in some obvious manner would permit him to reverse his image problem. He made a public apology in uniform from the Pentagon for inserting himself into politics with the photo.[34]

With Biden as president in June 2021, during sworn testimony to Congress, Miley stated that he believed it was important to understand "white rage." When pressed on his beliefs, Milley dismissed concerns, calling it offensive to call military officers and non-commissioned officers "woke."[35] Once again, dismissing that Critical Race Theory (CRT) and other Diversity, Equity, and Inclusion (DEI) policies were damaging the force, Milley got the media sound bite that made his image rebrand complete.

General Milley has done great damage to the troops. He sets a horrible example for those serving as well as those considering joining. After questions arose about his behavior with his Chinese counterpart, a Pentagon spokesman said it was in Milley's job description to do what he did—and therefore, he could not be held accountable.[36] Perhaps his staff should hand him a copy of the Goldwater Nichols Act[37] or DOD Directive 5100.1[38] that clearly define the chairman of the Joint Chiefs of Staff's job description. It doesn't mention discussing removing nuclear launch strike ability or military action from the control of an elected president, nor warning adversaries of US military action.

Additionally, in 2021, after the fall of Afghanistan, General Milley called the drone strike on an innocent family of ten "righteous."[39] Where's the accountability for being completely wrong on a military level, which certainly *is* part of Milley's job description?

Sadly, there is a double standard for those at the top versus those who actually fight in wars. Generals and senior officials have special immunity for failure, whereas others at lower ranks are constantly made examples for actions that are minor in comparison and usually don't get people killed. In contrast to the generals and high-level officials who face little to no scrutiny or accountability, the same treatment doesn't exist for those in lower-level positions who do a fraction of the damage. It's an officer's responsibility to tell the truth. Yet officers who uphold that obligation face the consequences of taking on the largest and most powerful government agency, the Department of Defense. Some bravely go forward, but they pay for it with their careers.

In 2007, in a rare critique, Lieutenant Colonel Paul Yingling, an Army commander and Iraq War veteran, published an article outlining leadership failures of military generals, their mismanagement of the Iraq War, and their inability to prepare the military for war, and compared the Iraq War to America's failures in Vietnam. Despite friends and colleagues advising against it, he refused to publish the article anonymously. LTC Yingling went on to say that the "intellectual and moral failures" of US generals would cause a crisis within the military. He wrote, "These debacles are not attributable to individual failures, but rather to a crisis in an entire institution: America's general officer corps. America's generals have failed to prepare our armed forces for war and advise civilian authorities on the application of force to achieve the aims of policy. . . . For the second time in a generation, the United States faces the prospect of defeat at the hands of an insurgency." He continued in a now-famous quote: "A private who loses a rifle suffers far greater consequences than a general who loses a war."[40]

As expected, the article was wildly popular and controversial. For years it remained sought-after reading for young officers. But there was an eerie silence from the top. While Yingling was still at Fort Hood, Texas, the base commander, General Jeff Hammond, brought around two hundred young captains together for a meeting, and while he never mentioned LTC Yingling's name, he ranted about how infuriated he was that someone who had never been a general felt that he could criticize the way generals do their jobs. He spoke of how inappropriate the article was. Yingling was selected to be a battalion commander before publishing his controversial article and went on to complete his third deployment in Iraq. He was later selected for promotion to colonel but was assigned to teach at the Marshal Center in Germany, an assignment usually considered a dead end for further promotion, and it was known Yingling would not make general. He ended up retiring as a colonel in rank, but a lieutenant colonel in pay grade.[41] Yingling stepped out of line by outing himself as a critical thinker and truth-teller. Once that happens, you're blacklisted and eventually not welcome in the general club. The irony is, with his outspoken and bold nature, Colonel Yingling probably would have made a great general. Qualities like those, coupled with having the intestinal fortitude to speak truth to power, are completely and utterly lacking in today's general corps, but are reminiscent of the World War II–era generals who earned the right to lead our nation's sons and daughters.

In 2021, Space Force commander, Air Force Academy graduate, fighter pilot, and instructor Lieutenant Colonel Matthew Lohmeier, whose job at the time was to detect ballistic missile strikes, was fired for speaking out about how the military is forcing Marxist ideological indoctrination through the ranks. He stated this during a podcast while promoting his book *Irresistible Revolution: Marxism's Goal of Conquest & the Unmaking of the American Military*. Lohmeier covered topics such as diversity and inclusion policies, the DOD-wide extremism stand-down day, and the Air Force's new plan to diversify the pilot corps.[42]

Lohmeier met with Air Force legal and public affairs officers beforehand to let them know he was publishing a book, and he took their advice on the process. They told him that he could consult with the office of prepublication and security review at the Pentagon but that it was not a required action in order to publish a book.[43]

Soon after the podcast, Lieutenant General Stephen Whiting, commander of Space Operations at Buckley Air Force Base, fired Lt. Col. Lohmeier for "loss of confidence in his ability to lead."[44] The military also tried to make the case that he had violated DOD Directive 1344.10, Political Activities by Members of the Armed Forces. The directive states that service members on active duty are not permitted to "participate in any radio, television, or other program or group discussion as an advocate for or against a partisan political party, candidate, or cause."[45]

Senator Roger Wicker, a Republican from Mississippi, took issue with DOD's lack of due process and hypocrisy surrounding Lt. Col. Lohmeier's treatment and sent a letter to Secretary of Defense Lloyd Austin. "If the Department of Defense finds that Lt. Col. Lohmeier's statements on CRT qualify as a 'partisan cause,' it would then follow that the Department recognizes CRT itself as reflecting one side in a partisan debate. Yet if CRT is partisan, it must be asked why this ideology is increasingly being pushed on US service members. It has become increasingly clear that the Department is actively pushing CRT through 'diversity and inclusion' trainings,[1] recommended reading materials,[2] and cadet instruction.[3] The Department therefore cannot call Lt. Col. Lohmeier's statements on CRT 'partisan' without being implicated in the same partisan advocacy."[46]

Lohmeier didn't participate in any sort of partisan political discussion. He spoke about the dangers of CRT in the military. That's it. One podcast, and he was out. Meanwhile, Mark Milley did an interview with Watergate journalist Bob Woodward who then divulged that Milley confessed to his Chinese counterpart that he would give him a heads up prior to President Trump's authorizing a military strike against China—and nothing happened to Milley. Nothing. That's the double standard. Talk facts about where the military is headed after giving your base public affairs office notice about your book? *Fired!* America's top general trying to circumvent the President of the United States with phones calls to China? *Safe!* It is a two-tiered justice system where those who dare to speak the politically incorrect truth face the harshest punishments.

In 2021, Marine Lieutenant Colonel Stuart Scheller, who had been serving for seventeen years, was charged, held in the brig (the military's version of jail), and later fired for making multiple videos that went viral online where he was critical of the way leadership handled the withdrawal from Afghanistan. While not one general who actually was responsible for the Afghanistan withdrawal debacle has been held accountable, Lt. Col. Scheller, who called for accountability of senior leaders' mismanagement of the war, was. He was charged with six violations of the Uniform Code of Military Justice (UCMJ), fired from his job as a battalion commander at Camp Lejeune, North Carolina, issued a gag order (to stop him from vocalizing his treatment and allow the Marine Corps the upper hand in controlling the narrative to the public), and was thrown in jail. He ended up pleading guilty to a special court-martial consisting of:

- Article 133: One count for conduct unbecoming an officer and a gentleman.
- Article 89: Four counts for disrespect toward superior commissioned officers.
- Article 90: One count for willfully disobeying a superior commissioned officer.
- Article 92: Dereliction in the performance of duties
- Article 92: Failure to obey order or regulation.
- Article 88: One count of contempt toward officials.[47]

He had to refund $5,000 worth of pay and resign from the Marines. He also received a letter of reprimand.[48] Scheller's video was quickly labeled as political, but it was not. Scheller merely told the truth about the inept handling of the Afghanistan War by senior leaders—which led to the worst foreign policy disaster since the end of the Vietnam War—and in doing so, he gave a voice to many service members and veterans who felt let down and abandoned by the military and the service for which they had risked everything. Scheller paid the price.

In the age of TikTok and Instagram, where service members constantly go to air their grievances about military lifestyle, policy, and deployments, Scheller's video hit with an air of authenticity. He was a lieutenant colonel and battalion commander with just shy of two decades in the Marines Corps. He clearly had a very promising career ahead of him. Scheller was almost there, nearly one of the made-men crowd—a senior leader much closer to the top than a standard service member airing grievances on social media. He was far enough along in his career that by the current standards he should have already committed to falling in line. Instead, Scheller's message resonated with the American public's experience of the twenty-year Afghanistan War. Scheller's viral videos exposed the truth that most outside of military ranks never get to experience firsthand. The Marine Corps did not appreciate the exorbitant amount of free publicity it was getting, especially considering how close this truth-dump hit home for Marine leadership. And so the Marine Corps threw the book at Scheller and made an extreme example of him. To this day, Lt. Col. Scheller is the only person who has been held accountable for anything surrounding the Afghanistan withdrawal. What is the message to the American public and the military? It's that as a senior leader you can completely screw up the operational planning and make a hash of an entire war, you can be incompetent in ensuring the tactical security of a base and the soldiers and civilians near it, and you can be sloppy and rushed enough to strike the wrong truck, killing innocent civilians—all without retribution. But if you dare speak out against any of those leaders and their heinous decisions, then you are the one that will be punished.

Rising commanders get the book thrown at them when they speak the truth, take a stand on principle, and raise the red flag on the failures from the Pentagon. Yet for senior leaders like Lloyd Austin and General Milley who lose entire wars, get innocents killed, mislead Congress and the American people, and downplay the reality of the wars, and those serving (and in Milley's case, speak out against the President of the United States—at the time, President Trump), there is no accountability. In fact, in many cases, those men are praised. The Pentagon circles the wagon in defense. The double standard continues.

The truth about today's generals is that the majority don't make it to where they are because they are stellar intellectuals who have the ability to strategize and win wars. They make it to the top because they play the appeasement game, don't vocalize problems, keep their readiness trackers green, and take the right general aide jobs. That's how you become a general today. You play the game, and you outlast. Of course, some generals are the exception. They are phenomenal, elite leaders who stay and sacrifice because they want to make the military, the nation, and the world a better and safer place. But sadly, those are few and far between.

Once these leaders get into a position of authority, they use their power to silence and fire anyone who dares speak the truth about the military's direction. Any disagreement or critical claim publicly is instantly seen as a threat—one that Pentagon leadership feels must be countered with the force and power of the Department of Defense.

That's precisely why, after January 6, 2021, Secretary Austin mandated his military commanders to conduct a force-wide stand-down day to combat extremism.[49] They took a handful of people affiliated with the military on January 6 and used them as an example to label all people who looked like them—primarily white men—as some sort of dangerous extremists.

One Army soldier I spoke with on the condition of anonymity described this "stand-down" from the inside and the conversations that ensued surrounding it. In early 2021, after January 6, a two-star general from the Pentagon visited his former special forces unit. This military unit was still in the middle of combat deployments throughout the world. The group was at that moment in harm's way. These are service members who are still getting shot at on deployments and face real, tangible threats from real malign actors that are actively plotting against our nation. When the general arrived, he was well received, and the unit was happy to host him.

When he arrived and sat down with the soldiers for their discussion, he started talking about how significant the domestic terrorism threat was, how it was the biggest threat to the military and our nation, and how dangerous this uprising of white supremacists in the military had become. The talk was confusing to the organization, as every intelligence report they read did not highlight this so-called growing terrorist threat but spoke of the looming dangers of near-peer adversaries, Russia and China. One of the soldiers finally interrupted the general's rant about how domestic terrorism was the number one threat to national security and said, "Sir, we see the threats we face around the world from violent extremism, and I thought the Pentagon was focusing on near-peer threats. I just don't see what you are talking about with this domestic extremism."

The general immediately went on defense: "Well, you don't see the intelligence that I do, and it is very much a real threat. Trust me, it's real."

These soldiers had the highest levels of security clearances. This man had asked a legitimate question. The general didn't have answers. Instead, he used his rank to try to make the soldier appear stupid for asking.

An officer chimed in, "Since this is such a significant and serious threat, are we looking at using the military to combat this domestic threat?" The general immediately downplayed it: "No, no, that's not where this is going. That's not going to happen."

In fact, he had no idea what he was talking about. It was obvious he was merely restating talking points from the Pentagon.

Soon thereafter, the soldier attended the DOD's mandatory force-wide stand-down day for extremism and domestic terrorism. After the presentation, a member of the organization asked his commander, "If domestic terrorism is really that bad, why aren't you also discussing the violence and anarchism that occurred in the summer of 2020, which was an order of magnitude more than what happened on January 6?" A question many members of the military still want an answer to.

Pentagon press secretary John Kirby went on to contradict the general's dramatic talk about extremism, saying that the Pentagon didn't actually know the extent of the domestic extremism, it was something they were looking into, and the "problem was likely greater than zero, but also likely not as large as some would speculate."[50]

Eventually the Countering Extremist Activity Working Group found "cases of prohibited extremist activity among service members were rare."[51] The military is comprised of 1.3 million active duty and over eight hundred thousand reserve and National Guard forces. They found one hundred cases of alleged extremism activity throughout the entire force.[52] For that, the Pentagon spent 5,359,000 hours on extremism prevention and $500,000 on the actual stand down.[53] Aside from the cost of taking a day away from training and preparing to be ready to take the fight to our nation's real enemies that exist, they took an entire day to tell those who voluntarily signed up to fight and potentially die for this nation that they, the warfighters themselves, were the problem.

There is still plenty of damage to be done. The culture rot runs too deep in military leadership across all services. Unfortunately, the reality is that the only accountability that will make any sort of meaningful change is to fire a considerable number of generals. Perhaps all of them. No more former generals as Secretary of Defense. No more leaders who have served on boards of the military-industrial complex. Clean house. Start from scratch. Is our military institution still salvageable? Maybe—but until Congress and senior civilian leadership get serious about real accountability instead of selective accountability, things will get much worse before they get better.

CHAPTER 3

The Cost of Freedom

*"Those who expect to reap the blessing of freedom must
undertake to support it."*

Thomas Paine

Young, healthy, able-bodied men and women don't want to serve in the military today. And it's hard to imagine why they would. For generations, Americans joined the military and placed their life on the line, knowing that they may have to die to defend our nation. American culture had a sense of pride in the nation's values and way of life and understood that it had to be protected. There was a certain level of patriotism in our nation that was mainstream. Americans loved freedom and backed the destruction of any enemy that was trying to take that away from our country. But that's long gone. That love of country and pride have been replaced with discontent from much of America's youth for the very freedoms that allow them to enjoy the American way of life. When Americans as a whole no longer feel freedoms are worth preserving, but believe that America and capitalism are the problem and the oppressor, then the nation is in for a rude adjustment.

After 9/11 many Americans felt a call to serve. It was a genera-tion's Pearl Harbor: the military saw a significant surge in recruitment following the 9/11 attacks, the biggest increase in enlistment since December 1941. Approximately 181,500 people joined the active duty military in the first year following 9/11, and 72,908 joined the Reserves. The Department of Defense registered an 8 percent increase in curiosity about the military in American youth wishing to serve their country.[1]

On September 10, 2001, Ian Patterson was a graduate student studying abroad in Australia. His mind was far from the military, war, or serving in any capacity. The military had never been something he thought he'd pursue. But when he watched the attacks of 9/11 unfold on a pub television, that all changed in an instant. To him, it wasn't New York City, it was *his* country. "I was the only foreigner in the pub. All of the Australians looked at me oddly. It was really overwhelming. I knew it was my time. It was my time to go home and do my part."

The next day he walked into the US embassy, and four months later was in the US as a direct enlistee, all because of the effects 9/11 had on him. He enlisted in the Air Force as a Combat Weather Forecaster and went on to deploy multiple times to Iraq and Afghanistan, as well as multiple NASA assignments. He left the military as a Staff Sergeant in 2009, earlier than expected due to medical reasons. The military taught him a higher level of discipline and gave direction to his life. His best days in the military were during his deployments, where he was the first weather forecaster in the eastern region of Afghanistan and where he got to work directly with units.

But when recently asked if he would promote military service to his children or anyone else he knew, he said, "No." He went on to say that it saddened him to admit it, but that he has even encouraged some teenagers of his friends who were interested in serving not to do so because of the current climate and culture within the military.

Once the reality of the wars hit the front page of the news, once the memory of the attacks from way back in 2001 faded and the initial fear of terrorism became an everyday part of America's life, the recruiting bump vanished.

In June 2005, the Army reported active duty recruitment numbers from October 2004 to June 2005, citing that it enlisted 47,121 soldiers. That is 14 percent, or 8,000 soldiers, short of meeting its numbers. Worse was that the National Guard reported missing its recruitment goals by 10,400 soldiers, a 23-percent shortage. And the Reserve's weren't far behind them. The Reserve reported missing its goal by 4,100, a 21-percent shortage.[2]

At the time, the military needed to maintain a force of 140,000 ground troops in Iraq to fight the war.[3] It needed an increase in recruits in order to continue to ship people off to Iraq. And by then, the war in Afghanistan was heating up again. At home, the economy was booming and jobs were expanding. Unemployment was down to 5 percent, and people had many options.[4] The patriotic 9/11 bump was gone.

Furthermore, the quality of those who did enlist was slipping. In the first nine months of fiscal year 2004, nearly 97 percent of Army recruits had graduated from high school. By June of 2005, high school diplomas from recruits had dropped to 89.3 percent. Test scores also dropped by 7.4 percent.[5]

Young Americans saw the realities of war. They saw deaths reported on the daily news, the separation from family, deployments lasting a year at a time, multiple back-to-back deployments, and young wounded soldiers returning home.

An all-volunteer force comes with its set of challenges. The post 9/11 military didn't have the luxury of conscription the way the military did in Vietnam.

So what did the Army do? It instituted the Stop-Loss policy, an involuntary force management program. Stop-Loss prevents service members from retiring or separating from the military at their previously agreed-upon date of exiting the military. As a former soldier during this time, I saw firsthand the serious toll the Stop-Loss policy took on the morale of the force. Many service members felt there was a double standard: they were required to uphold their end of their commitment, but the military could shift their contract dates when it felt doing so was necessary.

By 2007 the Army was enticing new recruits with significant signing bonuses. One of its programs between July and September 2007 was a $20,000 "quick ship" bonus that meant recruits had to ship out to basic training by September with the goals of helping the military meet its fiscal year end recruiting numbers.[6]

The Army also dropped its standards. One example: The Army granted a 65 percent increase in criminal waivers for recruits.[7] The Iraq surge strategy forced the Army recruiting command to get more creative and to drop standards even further. And it was clear to the force. Individuals that would have otherwise never been able to serve started showing up to join units in Iraq. Individuals that were overweight—even for normal civilian standards—individuals that had criminal pasts, some with tattoos on their necks and faces, arrived.

A few years later, recruiting numbers stabilized, but people who joined the military were not doing so out of patriotism elicited by the terrorist attacks.[8] Most wanted a job, even more so if it came with a significant bonus. And there is nothing wrong with that—serving your country is serving your country, regardless of motivation.

As the war in Iraq wound down, both due to official combat operations ceasing and political and diplomatic disagreements between the United States and the new government of Iraq, the military's primary focus turned back towards Afghanistan. But by this point, Osama bin Laden was dead.

The Taliban was still there and still very much willing to fight. But if we hadn't defeated them in over a decade, how many more years would make a difference? How many more American deaths? How much money thrown at the problem would suffice?

People were starting to pay attention, service members included. With the change in the media landscape, service members were getting their news in real time, even downrange during deployments. They saw the stark contrast between what was being said in Washington by Pentagon spokespeople, DOD officials, other national security officials, and military brass versus what they were witnessing on the ground in Iraq and Afghanistan. It didn't seem to them that the Afghanistan military was capable of standing on its own two feet without being propped by the US military and funded by the American taxpayer.

There seemed to be no one who could actually articulate what the US military was still doing in Afghanistan. Osama bin Laden's death was in 2011, but Americans were still being killed nearly a decade later.[9] We kept hearing the same old story: "We're allowing girls to go to school." "We're providing Afghans with a future free from terrorists." "We're fighting them there so we don't have to fight them here." The war went on and on and on and on. Many Americans finally started to grow weary and ask questions. But those who dared speak up were often smeared as un-American or as isolationists who didn't support the troops.

Bureaucracy doesn't know how to innovate or change. The status quo is easier than change. Plus, generals and near-generals who no longer fight in actual wars would not have the same post-military opportunities without the war. A wartime general just has a better ring to it than a general who merely trains troops for war. And since the war didn't carry any consequences for those who were responsible for them, why make any changes? The war was job security that led to cushy board seats on the defense primes, becoming heads of universities, or even obtaining presidential cabinet seats. War was a ladder to be climbed.

Despite those failures, despite Americans still dying, despite the unaccounted taxpayer funds, despite the lies told as proven by the Afghanistan Papers, those generals were promoted.[10] In today's military, you fail up. You get rewarded for keeping your mouth shut, for toeing the line, and for being a follower. The World War II generals are no more.

Today's generals have given up on remaining apolitical. Generals now serve political agendas over leading and caring for troops.

Without the Iraq and Afghanistan Wars, the military faced an identity crisis. The wars were all the military had known for nearly two decades. They were its purpose to devote time, energy, and efforts to, but they gave the entire institution a false sense of security when it came to preparing for real near-peer adversaries. While the military fought terrorists with AK-47s in the mountains of Afghanistan and the deserts of Iraq, China was playing the long game. China was building companies like TikTok and Huawei cell phones to attempt to infiltrate the US government.

Our nation's soldiers and would-be recruits saw all of this. They paid attention. And they voted with their pens. Many signed DD214s (the document you receive when you exit the military) sooner than they otherwise would have.

Today, the military is faced with recruiting a new generation: one that was born after the 9/11 attacks. Some learn about 9/11 at school, others recognize it as a historical remembrance day for an event that no longer impacts their world.

Only about 23 percent of Americans aged seventeen to twenty-four are eligible for military service. The 77 percent that are ineligible are mostly due to obesity, other disqualifying medical conditions, drug use, and criminal records. In May 2022, Army chief of staff General

James McConville testified in front of Congress that of Americans aged seventeen to twenty-four, only 23 percent are qualified to do so without some sort of a waiver. And that is down considerably from the last few years. According to NBC News, only 9 percent of qualified Americans would be willing to consider military service as a path for their future.[11] That is a startling slap in the face to the military that spends billions on recruitment annually.

While the military points to these numbers as an excuse for the current recruitment and retention crisis, they are not telling the whole story. The obesity problem has been an issue for decades. The COVID-19 vaccine mandate was self-inflicted—military leadership chose to kick people out who had religious, moral, or medical objections. The civ-mil divide has been widening for decades and is not a new problem. Despite these issues, in recent years, the military has still been able to meet its recruiting requirements (or come close) and hold its force strength end-state while only being able to pull from the 23–29 percent of qualified Americans. But no more. The issue today is that the military has lost the 23 percent due to an increasingly political military whose priorities follow social trends, and the failed leadership that enforces those trends.

Young Americans are smart, they are all connected through social media, and they are well informed. They have taken notice of what today's military culture is actually about. They see in real time the problems that plague the military today. They see the news headlines and the social media videos about how soldiers and their families make so little money that the Army advises them to utilize food stamps.[12] There are TikTok and social media posts that have gone viral from service members who air their grievances. They see senior level military leaders being dramatic and unprofessional on social media and harming the military's already waning reputation.

Major General Patrick Donahoe, the former commander of Maneuver Center of Excellence at Fort Benning, Georgia, home of Ranger School, the Army's premier leadership school, first made headlines in March 2021. The general thought it was his place to counter a media segment from Fox News host Tucker Carlson, who called out the military for becoming soft and losing focus of the mission by catering to women with new hairstyles and flight suits for pregnant women. In response, General Donahoe tweeted a video of himself re-enlisting a female soldier with a caption that read, "Just a reminder that @ TuckerCarlson couldn't be more wrong."[13] Other military leaders followed by tweeting support for the general.

General Paul Funk felt the need to chime in and tweeted, "I agree Pat. Thousands of women serve honorably every day around the globe. They are beacons of freedom and they prove Carlson wrong through determination and dedication. We are fortunate they serve with us."[14]

That tweet led to a response from the Sergeant Major of the Army: "Women lead our most lethal units with character. They will dominate ANY future battlefield we're called to fight on. @ TuckerCarlson's words are divisive, don't reflect our values. We have THE MOST professional, educated, agile, and strongest NCO Corps in the world."[15]

Seems a bit unprofessional to have senior military leaders triggered by civilian media personalities. It was also incredibly, needlessly politically divisive. Additionally, the response came off as creepy—as if women need a general to stand up for them because they can't do it themselves. This was certainly counter to the Army's narrative of women being completely equal to men in the military. Of course, these senior leaders totally missed the point Carlson was making, which was that considerable time and treasure had been spent by the Army on matters such as accommodating women's ponytails.

Pentagon spokesperson John Kirby also felt the need to justify women serving. He started by saying that the military "won't take personnel advice from a talk show host or the Chinese military." He went on to say, "A major and specific contributor to that advantage are the women who serve: civilian and military alike. . . . And today they serve in just about every skill set we put to sea and in the field. They're flying fighter jets and commanding warships. They're leading troops on the ground. They're making a difference in everything we do because of what they bring to the effort."[16] Again, not the point. Everyone knows that women are serving in the military.

Senator Ted Cruz took issue with military leadership engaging and instigating social media drama and sent a letter to Secretary of Defense Lloyd Austin. "This spectacle risks politicizing the military after several centuries of efforts to keep military officials out of domestic affairs, undermining civil-military relations by having the military take a side in a contentious cultural dispute and the perception that military leaders are happily weaponizing the institution against political critics of the sitting administration," Senator Cruz wrote.[17] This prompted an Army investigation into General Donahoe's conduct.

But four months later, the general was at it again. This time, he took to Twitter to disparage an Army veteran and Hillsdale college student who had a differing opinion on the military's mandatory COVID vaccine policy. "Hey @Hillsdale come get your boy," the general tweeted after an unprofessional Twitter exchange. When a Twitter user then asked him how many wars he had won, the general replied, "don't be a shill for Putin."[18]

When young Americans are thinking about joining the military and see this exchange on a national stage, they may think twice about joining after seeing the type of leadership they will have to serve under. And just as bad, their parents may have seen that behavior and said, "Absolutely not." Recruits don't want woke generals. They want leaders who will lead them to victory on the battlefield, who will look out for them, not those that get their feelings hurt over an opinion news show segment.

The military must wake up to the fact that it is competing for the 9 percent of eligible young Americans who may actually be interested in such a profession. What motivates them? Shooting guns, patriotism, protecting the country, paying for college, a sense of adventure, and getting to drive or work on cool equipment or technology. Not mandatory training on social issues that are not applicable to their everyday jobs and service. Or being told that if they are a specific skin color or gender, they are likely an extremist. Not having to fill out form after form to go on leave or pass. Those things have a tendency to drive people away from service.

We have an all-volunteer force. If we want to keep it that way, the military must stop making it so painful to serve. It took the Army twenty-seven years to update their DA Form 31,[19] which is the Request and Authority for Leave form, the paperwork that every soldier must fill out to go home to see his or her parents, girlfriend, boyfriend, to take paid vacation days, or even to go on a honeymoon. It's a form that gets used daily, was incredibly painful to use, and was extremely outdated.

All of the good and fun parts of the military—the reasons for most wanting to join in the first place—have been steadily replaced with misery. Of course America's youth don't want to join the military. It has substituted fighting and killing the enemy with sensitivity training. When I was in the military, it was fun and purposeful. It was professional. It was focused on wars and the mission and training to ensure we had the best chance at coming home alive from our deployments. But the job itself was frequently engaging and simply fun to do.

It used to be that veterans and service members could be counted on to be primary recruiters. Any time veterans spoke about their time in the military, they would usually promote it. The military had become, in effect, a family business. Those days are done.

This crisis of military leadership did not come without consequences. The Afghanistan War withdrawal, politicized leadership, and woke policies have had a detrimental effect on not only recruitment, but retention. While we've already seen the numbers for the detrimental recruitment crisis emerge in 2022, the retention crisis will be a bit more subtle, but equally as horrible for the force. Right now, experienced combat veterans of all types are riding out the time left on their contract or to their retirement date. Many will not be replaced.

I spoke to one Army officer, a West Point graduate and special operator, who has done multiple deployments to the Middle East. He was a higher performer with top blocks on all of his OERs. Yet he "is counting down the days" until he can get out. He said that he doesn't recognize the military that he once loved anymore and that he knows he is a political pawn for war-hungry politicians in D.C. Two years ago, this man turned down battalion command. Battalion command is something that officers work towards their entire career. It is supposed to be the highest honor and distinction an officer can have. At West Point, it is taught that being selected for battalion command means success—with the implication that not striving for battalion command makes you a sub-standard leader. It was hard for him to turn the assignment down. It meant rethinking everything he had worked for since his first days at West Point. It was a hard pill to swallow. But now he had been deployed nonstop since the early days of the Iraq War, and he was tired of life in an Army that had worked him at a non-healthy cadence. Battalion command would have meant two more years of an intense pace with no work-life balance. And for what? Guaranteed inspector general complaints against you, getting flagged because of those investigations, and pushing tired soldiers to do more. But he'd work for more pay, right? No. There is no pay incentive for battalion commanders.

They are paid exactly as those of the same rank who have cushy staff jobs in Tampa or Hawaii. For this soldier, it was no longer worth it. Being away from family. Prioritizing the Army over every other aspect of his life. There was no reward for battalion command.

Unfortunately, this man's story isn't rare. Good officers are getting out, turning down battalion commands, moving on. The writing is on the wall. No matter how much or how hard they work, they will get the exact same paycheck and retirement as the officer that goes to online grad school on his work computer. There is no incentive structure to work hard or advance. And those who do work hard get frustrated as they see undeserving peers get early promotion due to a broken system, or get the exact same pay for a quarter of the work. Those officers start to look for opportunities elsewhere, where they are competitive and where their abilities and experience are valued. Those who stay reap the benefits of the talented leaving. They get promoted. They get commands. The best and the brightest have choices. They are tired of a military they no longer recognize. They are tired of politics and having to play the game to succeed. If the one conviction that was keeping them going was patriotic duty to serve—well, it's no wonder the retention crisis continues to grow.

We haven't seen this level of recruitment failure in nearly fifty years. It could not come at a more dangerous time, and it will only get worse. The American people have gotten comfortable with an all-volunteer military. But they should not get used to it. Considering the way the American political and military leadership like to get involved in wars, most should be extremely nervous, especially if they have a high school–aged son.

CHAPTER 4

Silencing Dissent

"Those who don't know the value of loyalty can never appreciate the cost of betrayal."
Unknown

The Department of Defense COVID vaccine mandate was detrimental to the force. It lasted almost a year and a half and became a self-inflicted national security threat to readiness, recruitment, and retention, as well as a nationwide disgrace. Secretary Austin threw away all sense of reason and kicked out thousands of battle-tested service members with years of priceless combat and leadership experience. Mind you, his decision to throw away these proficient service members coincided with the biggest recruitment crisis since Vietnam. The consequences of this foolish and ego-driven decision will be felt for years. It caused irreversible damage to morale, the military's reputation, and recruitment and retention.

In March 2021, prior to the vaccine mandate, Austin said that "defeating COVID-19 is the greatest proximate challenge to our nation's security."[1] Since then, matters escalated. Secretary Austin seemed to forget that the service members he commanded actually had excellent critical thinking skills of their own and the courage to stand up to policies they thought unjust, unfair, and illegal.

On August 9, 2021, Austin sent a memo to the force indicating his intent to make the vaccine mandate mandatory by mid-September or earlier if the US Food and Drug Administration (FDA) received its licensure. He encouraged all DOD employees and service members not to wait for the mandate but to get vaccinated immediately. He assured the force that the vaccines were safe: "All FDA-authorized COVID-19 vaccines are safe and highly effective. They will protect you and your family. They will protect your unit, your ship, and your co-workers. And they will ensure we remain the most lethal and ready force in the world. Get the shot. Stay healthy. Stay ready."[2]

But by August 23, 2021, earlier than expected, the FDA announced that it had approved the Pfizer-BioNTech COVID-19 vaccine for those sixteen and older. The very next day, the Pentagon sent out another memo to the force stating the COVID vaccine was now required for all service members. "To defend this Nation, we need a healthy and ready force," it read. "After careful consultation with medical experts and military leadership, and with the support of the President, I have determined that mandatory vaccination against coronavirus disease 2019 (COVID-19) is necessary to protect the force and defend the American people." The memo continued, "Those with previous COVID-19 infection are not considered fully vaccinated."[3]

Division commanders went all-in on mandatory enforcement. Leaders accepted the narrative at face value and dismissed service members' personal concerns. Once an order comes down from the division or brigade commander, lower-level leadership falls in line. Leaders went into execution mode. Overnight, COVID vaccinations became the military's number one priority. Officers knew if they wanted an excellent Officer Evaluation Report, their yearly performance evaluation, they had to show how seriously they were taking COVID and what measures they were taking to ensure their unit, battalion, brigade, company, etc., had the best COVID numbers. Refusals and exemptions made commanders look bad on paper and came with intense judgment and criticism from peers and senior commanders alike.

The Pentagon used what turned out to be White House propaganda to push the vaccine as safe and effective. Austin also said that the "job" of administering the mandate would be handled with compassion. This was not the case. Thousands of service members were treated as lepers and outcasts; they were black-balled, flagged, threatened, intimidated, disrespected, passed over for jobs, degraded, and forced to wear the scarlet letter of a mask—the policy for service members if they had not been vaccinated. The service members who doubted the efficacy and safety of the vaccine were challenged with a very difficult decision; on one hand, if they did not take the vaccine, they knew they would likely get kicked out of the military. This meant not being able to afford to pay rent, put food on the table, or save for their kids' college. Some were even told they might have to pay back their signing bonuses.[4]

On the other hand, they were unsure if they should put an unproven vaccine in their body without knowing the potential long-term impacts. This population of service members felt like they had no choice but to chance a dangerous, unproven vaccine over losing their livelihood. For those exact reasons, thousands of people who didn't want to take the vaccine nevertheless took it.

Some were exempt automatically. Those service members within six months of separation or retirement were granted administrative accommodation, meaning they were not required to take the shot.[5] This administrative loophole to the vaccine mandate highlighted to the rest of the military the inconsistencies with the COVID-19 vaccine policy. Military leaders told service members that they had to take the shot to help slow the spread of the virus, yet people on their way out of the service shortly somehow couldn't spread it. Those who were

"out-processing" from the military and never got the vaccine still inter-
acted daily with the rest of their units who were vaccinated. Military
leaders obviously were not worried about them spreading the virus
due to their lack of a vaccination. They were keeping up appearances.

Service members who were participating in the clinical trial of the
COVID vaccine were also "exempted from mandatory vaccination
against COVID-19 until the trial is complete in order to avoid invali-
dating such clinical trial results," as stated in Secretary Austin's memo.[6]
So all of the service members who were participating in the trials and
received a placebo shot were not deemed as a threat to the fighting force
or able to spread the virus to other troops? If it were such a significant
danger to the force, why were they allowed to participate in the trial in
the first place? Again, there was no quarantine in place. Soldiers who
received a placebo shot were still interacting daily with their fellow
service members who received the shot.

Standard cases of COVID last around one to two weeks.
Transgenders undergoing transition, surgeries, therapies, and aftermath
profiles can be out of operational service anywhere from months to
years. This absence can severely damage readiness simply by how long
the service member will be out of training at home and unavailable to
fight. Transition plans are highly individualized and require considerable
time from commanders and medical personnel assisting with the plan.

It is expected to take around a year for someone on hormone
replacement therapy to reach the desired physiological state. Due to
some of those changes, especially near the beginning, transgenders who
take hormones can be placed on limited duty for weeks. If they have any
type of surgery, top, bottom, or cosmetic, they can be out for months.
Additionally, there are increased complications post-surgery that may
impact the requirement for follow-on care. It is easy to envision how
transitioning genders in the military might negatively affect readiness.
The DOD, however, maintains that there will be minimal readiness

impact.[7] The double standard is grotesque and obvious. "Readiness" becomes an adjustable scale depending on the cultural politics involved.

People took note. Tens of thousands of those wearing the uniform were suspicious of a brand-new vaccine. There was no long-term data. Everyone was supposed to just believe what the "experts" were saying. Leaders perceived questions as criticizing their leaders, failing to obey orders, or "not believing in science." The gaslighting was unbelievable. The government expected no one to do his own research or to ask his own questions.

To date, the COVID vaccine mandate has done far more to damage the readiness of the force than have service members contracting COVID. The COVID vaccine mandate eroded the special trust and confidence a generation of service members had in their commanders and senior leaders.

After the mandate, the lens through which men and women viewed what they were fighting for changed. Bureaucrats at the Pentagon clearly did not imagine that military members would resist the vaccine the way they did and, in doing so, defy the order. After all, mandatory vaccines have been required for the military as long as vaccines have been around. The problem is that the military has, until the recent past, taught young leaders to be critical thinkers, to stand up for their values, and to take the hard right over the easy wrong.

The military faced a damning dilemma: proceed with kicking out tens of thousands of service members across every branch, including National Guard and Reserves, or walk back the order. In a bizarre twist, the Pentagon doubled down. Amid the biggest recruiting crisis since the Vietnam War, they began ejecting healthy, capable, combat-experienced service members and leaders. Military leadership treated these people as if they were enemy combatants. Thousands of religious accommodations were denied. Many who submitted exemptions were placed in purgatory status—no one gave them an update on the status of their packets for months. The military went after their own people as if they were criminals.

In the end, the Pentagon says 8,400 able-bodied, experienced, and healthy service members were forced out.[8] But that number doesn't reflect the whole truth. The number affected is much higher than that because many service members were eligible to retire or for ETS, meaning their contract was up and they could get out at any time. These individuals fell into the category of leaving the service in six months or less and were no longer required to take the vaccine. This convenient circumstance kept the numbers of this PR nightmare down for the Pentagon. Plenty of soldiers said there was no way they would take the COVID shot and opted to drop their separation or retirement paperwork to get out as soon as possible. These are service members who otherwise would have stayed in the military. Ironically, one of the Army's core values is "moral courage."[9] And tens of thousands of service members were brave enough to stand up to the largest and most intimidating government agency of all and refuse to take the vaccine, whether for medical reasons, religious reasons, or personal reasons.

In addition to the question of efficacy, there were also serious questions regarding the legality surrounding the order. Many lawsuits were brought against the Department of Defense for ordering an unlawful vaccine mandate. Some service members had already contracted COVID and had natural immunity. The Department of Defense refused to acknowledge natural immunity as a reason to be exempt from the vaccine. One lawsuit stated that "service members that have natural immunity, developed from surviving the virus, should be granted a medical exemption from compulsory vaccination because the DOD instruction policy reflects the well-established understanding that prior infection provides the immune system's best possible response to the virus."[10]

Another portion of the lawsuit argued that the Department of Defense had used vaccine vials that were made and delivered to military units prior to the FDA approval of the COVID vaccine and were technically still under an emergency use authorization (EUA) from the FDA. These vials did not meet the criteria defined by law to be administered to the troops.[11] The Comirnaty vaccine had full FDA approval, and was therefore allowed to be used under the vaccine mandate, while the other vaccine, Pfizer-BioNTech, should not have been allowed to be administered to service members under the mandate. If service members voluntarily selected the Pfizer under the EUA, then that was their choice. But if the vaccine was mandated, then legally, they should only have been forced to take the Comirnaty shot.

Clearly, the military didn't want to waste the Pfizer shots they already had on hand or wait however long it would take to get the Comirnaty shots. While the FDA may say that Pfizer-BioNTech "can be used interchangeably to provide the COVID-19 vaccination series without presenting any safety or effectiveness concerns,"[12] the law says something different. In order for Secretary Austin to mandate the vaccine to the force, he had to wait until the FDA issued full approval; otherwise Austin would have to request a waiver from the president. Once the vaccine had fully licensed FDA approval, Austin could issue the order himself, without a waiver. The EUA vaccine could be taken voluntarily. The pre-approval versions of the Pfizer vaccine should not have been mandated.

Even Secretary Austin's vaccine mandate memo issued August 24, 2021, stated, "Mandatory vaccination against COVID-19 will only use COVID-19 vaccines that receive full licensure from the Food and Drug Administration (FDA), in accordance with FDA-approved labeling and guidance."[13] The issue was, once the mandate came out, military units were forcing service members to take the leftover, on-hand EUA vaccine instead of a fully licensed version of the vaccine. The lawsuit argued that the DOD wasn't following its own order by using the Pfizer-BioNTech vaccine that had been distributed as EUA. While some may argue it's a technicality, it indicates that the DOD was picking and choosing when they had to follow the rules while requiring service members to follow the rules without asking questions.

What the DOD didn't bet on was that thousands of service members would realize this legal inconsistency and file a lawsuit against the department.

Some women serving in the military who were pregnant were rightfully worried about taking a vaccine with no data and how it might affect the baby and the rest of their pregnancy. Additionally, people who were trying to conceive or wanted to in the future were worried about infertility. The lawsuit argued that the FDA did not consider pregnancy or natural immunity when they approved the vaccine for adults.[14]

There were also concerns regarding the military process for denying the thousands of religious accommodation requests, which by law, require individual assessments for determination. But an inspector general report found the opposite: There was "a trend of generalized assessments rather than the individualized assessment that is required by federal law and DoD and Military Service policies." The report continued: "[S]imilar, if not identical wording" was used in denial memos. It also stated that the Navy and Air Force did not "reflect an individualized analysis demonstrating that the Senior Military Official considered the full range of facts and circumstances relevant to the particular religious accommodation request."[15]

This is significant abuse of power from senior military officials. They had little regard for the law and seemed to be overtly flouting it by using identical form letters with name and unit inserted when denials were sent out to service members.

By December 2021, approximately four months after the mandate, roughly 99 percent of the active duty Air Force, Space Force, Navy, and Marines were vaccinated. The Army came in at a little less, at 98 percent. The National Guard and Reserve were around 90 percent.[16] Thousands of service members had requested religious and medical exemptions, and an even smaller group who didn't submit an exemption refused to get the shot.[17] The Pentagon went after the group that refused to comply with a direct and "lawful" order, and those individuals faced disciplinary action and discharge. While a small percentage of active duty resisted, the nation's Reserve and National Guard troops resisted in higher numbers—likely because they only work for the military part-time and have civilian jobs where they are accustomed to asserting rights and standing up for themselves.[18]

As of June 2022, about forty thousand National Guard members were unvaccinated with about twenty-two thousand Reserve members unvaccinated.[19] That is over sixty thousand troops whom the federal government counts on for national emergencies, national disasters like fires and hurricane response, as well as backfill for the active duty force during a time of war; all were on track to be kicked out of the service due to Austin's vaccine mandate. The Pentagon made it very clear that they were losing patience with the holdouts. John Kirby, Pentagon spokesperson, said, "It's our expectation that the chain of command for every Guardsman—just like the chain of command for every active-duty member of the armed forces . . . will manage the mandatory vaccine requirement appropriately. . . . If they don't, then they, too, can be held to account under the [Uniform Code of Military Justice] for failure to obey a lawful order." That was a clear message to National Guard commanders: get your troops under control and force them to get vaccinated, or you yourself will face the consequences. The Air Guard was given until the end of 2022 to get the vaccine, while the Army National Guard was given until June 2022.[20] Many had already lost pay, benefits, and priceless federal military training required for readiness.

At the end of 2022, 8,400 troops had been discharged for refusing to comply with the COVID vaccine mandate: 3,737 Marine, 2,041 Navy, 1,841 Army and 834 from the Air Force and Space Force.[21] Losing that many service members is a catastrophic blow to the military and its capabilities and readiness to defend our nation. Those that remained had to do more with fewer people. They saw their colleagues, friends, and brothers and sisters in arms treated poorly, as expendable. Morale plummeted.

By the summer of 2022, many Republican members of Congress had had enough with the detrimental effects of the mandate on the force. Congressman Mike Waltz (R-FL), along with forty-nine other representatives, sent a letter to the Pentagon saying, "As a matter of national security, the capabilities and readiness of the fighting force, and respect for the personal rights of our men and women in uniform, we ask that you reconsider the Department's COVID vaccine mandate. . . ."[22] They wanted Secretary Austin to reconsider natural immunity, something the DOD had refused to do. Congress finally took matters into its own hands with the defense bill, the National Defense Authorization Act.

As a result of the FY23 NDAA, signed into law on December 23, 2022, the COVID vaccine mandate was to be rescinded within thirty days. On January 10, 2023, Secretary Austin reluctantly sent a memo to the force officially revoking the order. Austin was unapologetic in his new memo about his initial order and patted himself on his back for his service, saying his mandate "will leave a lasting legacy in the many lives we saved, the world-class Force we have been able to field, and the high level of readiness we have maintained, amidst difficult public health conditions."[23]

Austin urged commanders to continue pushing the vaccine: "The Department will continue to promote and encourage COVID-19 vaccination for all service members. . . . Vaccination enhances operational readiness and protects the Force."[24] He went on to say that commanders are responsible for their troops' health and readiness and have the authority to decide whether or not unvaccinated troops should be allowed to deploy or conduct any foreign travel. Deployments are vital for promotions, awards, and helping a service member advance.

By contrast, note that as of June 2022, the DOD updated its HIV policy to state that service members with HIV were now no longer forced out of the military and were allowed to deploy,[25] after a federal judge ruled that the Pentagon's previous policy was discriminatory toward people with HIV.[26] The Biden administration did not appeal the court decision. Now, depending on the unit commander, a service member can deploy with HIV, but that same service member might be restricted from the same deployment if he or she does not have the COVID-19 vaccine.

Just weeks before the NDAA passed in December 2022, Secretary of the Navy Carlos Del Toro made a last-minute plea to retain the vaccine mandate. "Unquestionably, it will create almost two classes of citizens in our services: those that can't deploy and those that can deploy. And that creates all sorts of problems," he said. "Let's make sure we understand the secondary consequences of our actions."[27] That's of course exactly what the vaccine mandate had already accomplished.

By February 2023, the Navy quietly resolved its self-created problem, stating, "COVID-19 vaccination status shall not be a consideration in assessing individual service member suitability for deployment or other operational missions."[28]

Austin's memo also effectively resolved all exemptions from the vaccine mandate. Austin's memo said that those who had submitted exemptions but were denied *should* have their records updated to remove those denials and, if any adverse action was taken, including a letter of reprimand, *should* have it removed from their file.[29] Of course it will be the burden of the individual soldier to ensure that happens.

The memo went on to address the issue of those service members who were forced out and received a discharge for "disobeying a lawful order," either an honorable discharge or a general discharge under honorable conditions, as having the right to petition their military service to pursue a change in "characterization of their discharge" in their official records.[30] It did not address how long the process would take or how it would be listed. Discharges from the military for anything other than an honorable may affect the service member's veteran benefits and eligibility.

Despite the military denying almost all requests for religious exemptions, Austin made sure to include in the memo a remark on religious liberty. He stated that *all* service members have the right to observe their chosen religion and that the Department of Defense would continue to uphold and support religious liberty through the Armed Forces.[31] The hypocrisy was glaring. Of the tens of thousands who had requested religious exemptions, only a handful were granted. The Navy approved 1.02 percent of the religious exemptions. The Army approved 6.04 percent. The Air Force and Space Force approved 2.31 percent. The Marines only approved 0.52 percent.[32]

Despite the memo, questions remain as to whether those who submitted exemptions will still have some sort of identification letter in their personnel file marking them as disobedient, a status which could affect them in the future for job assignments, promotion, or other selection. In a House Armed Services personnel subcommittee on February 28, 2023, Under Secretary of Defense for Personnel Gilbert Cisneros Jr. testified that some service members who refused to take the vaccine and did not file for an exemption were still being pursued for punishment for "disobey[ing] a lawful order."[33] That's right: the Pentagon was using its resources to punish those service members who didn't get the vaccine.

In that same hearing, Cisneros revealed that the military was not reaching out to those 8,400 service members who had been forced out for reconciliation or to gauge interest in reenlistment: "[T]he policy is the same that has always been. If service members are discharged and they want to come back into the service, they can apply."[34]

The Pentagon doesn't want them back. It has divided the military into two classes: the vaccinated and the unvaccinated.

Fifty-four Air Force pilots were forced out for not taking the vaccine, either through separation or retirement. There is a massive pilot shortage in the Air Force. The service was 1,907 pilots short in 2021.[35] The financial cost of losing a pilot is significant, as well as the loss of priceless experience and leadership. The training costs are astronomical. It costs $7.3 million to train a B-1 pilot; $9.7 million to train a B-52 pilot; $10.9 million to train an F-22 pilot; $2.5 million to train a C-130J pilot.[36] The time required to train a pilot is significant as well. The cost is steep, and losses at scale are nearly unrecoverable. Instead, Pentagon leadership is treating the loss of fifty-four pilots in the force like pocket change.

It took the Secretary of the Army almost a month and a half to follow the Pentagon's lead and send a memo to the force that the vaccine was no longer a requirement for those serving or for potential recruits. Throughout the entire process of the military COVID vaccine requirements, senior military and civilian officials operated as though they were above the law and could pick and choose when and how they wanted to apply it—all while making the service members who stood up to them suffer for asserting rights guaranteed to them by the law.

As of December 2022, ninety-six active duty National Guard and Reserve service members have died from COVID illness since the COVID outbreak began in 2020.[37] The Department of Defense annual report on suicide in the military for 2021 stated that 519 service members died from suicide in 2021 alone. In 2020, a total of 582 service members lost their lives to suicide.[38] That's a total of 1,101 losses in two years, almost 11.5 times the rate of COVID deaths. But senior military leadership hasn't tackled the suicide issue the same way it tackled COVID.

One crisis is political, and one is not.

Secretary Austin chose to divide the force, because it was politically advantageous for him to do so. The Austin mandate is a stain on the US military and dishonored all those who have served and value the military.

David Hamski grew up in a family whose members had devoted their professional lives to serve as firefighters and paramedics, and he had uncles who served in the military. He loved playing Army as a kid. The attacks on our country on September 11, 2001, occurred when he was a fifth grader and had a lasting impact on him. His dad was a firefighter. For the first time, he saw that there was good and evil in this world and that evil must be opposed. He wanted to join the military. Over the years, he worked hard and never lost sight of this goal. In 2009, he was a new cadet at the United States Military Academy at West Point, nestled on the Hudson River in New York state. After four grueling years, he graduated in 2013 as a second lieutenant in the Infantry. He loved the Army and took advantage of every school he could get his hands on. He graduated from Ranger School, Ranger Instruction, Pathfinder, Senior-rated Jumpmaster, Mountaineer, Cold Weather Indoctrination Instructor, and earned his Expert Infantryman's badge. He went on operational deployments to Southeast Asia, including Thailand, South Korea, and the Philippines.

He loved being in the field, teaching other soldiers the profession of arms. Teaching students at Ranger school was his most formative experience. He relished in the responsibility and pressures of being an instructor to sixteen students during the Benning phase (also known as Darby phase), which lasted three arduous weeks. Ranger instructors were tasked with training and evaluating soldiers in the forested training area through brutal terrain, including swaps and deep erosion ditches. Students would approach him back at the base and tell him how impactful his teaching and example had been for them. He was selected for two infantry company commands—in comparison, few officers are granted even one. Captain Hamski was one of our nation's best. The pride of the infantry and, therefore, the Army. He was a successful, dedicated officer who bought into the mission and the values of his beloved US Army.

After successfully completing his first command, in April of 2021, Captain Hamski began his second command as the company commander for Headquarters Company (HHC) of 3rd Battalion, 509th Parachute Infantry Regiment of the 4th Brigade Combat Team, 25th Infantry Division (now reflagged as 2nd brigade, 11th Airborne Division) at Joint Base Elmendorf-Richardson near Anchorage, Alaska. Soon after he assumed his position, COVID hit. Around that same time, word got out that the COVID vaccine would be rolled out as soon as possible.

Hamski had an uneasy feeling about this. A lifelong learner and critical thinker, he had already done his own research. The entire process seemed rushed. He had a colleague who was on Operation Warp Speed, the government's accelerated vaccine project, who assured him it was safe. But he knew other vaccines normally require years of studies and tests before a vaccine goes to market.

In March of 2021, commanders at Joint Base Elmendorf-Richardson received a large batch of vaccines and started urging soldiers to get the jab. By then, Hamski had decided he wouldn't take the vaccine. He told his battalion commander that he wouldn't take it and shared his concerns with him. His commander said it would soon be mandatory, and while he understood Hamki's personal concerns, he would be required to follow the orders of the Army and the officers above him. Hamski saw then and there that his command would not go to bat for him. The pressure to take the vaccine continued from command sergeant major meetings to leaders' breakfasts. His S3 operations officer, a major (and the next higher rank), came up to him in the hallway in front of people, shook him by the shoulders, and said, "I'm trying to shake some sense into you."

The week the mandate memo was released by the Secretary of Defense, the unit had a brigade run. The brigade commander, a full-bird colonel, called all commanders and first sergeants to the middle of a field, and everyone gathered around him in a circle totaling about fifty people. The brigade commander looked around at everyone sternly and said, "You will all get the vaccine. I'm not screwing around." He said if they didn't, he would relieve them of command, get a relief for cause evaluation report, receive a General Officer Memorandum of Reprimand (GOMOR), and possibly request a dishonorable discharge.

The threats and coercion kept rolling in. Hamski was the only one in the circle who was vocal about not getting the shot, and everyone knew he refused to take it. The "talk" was clearly aimed at him. But the Army had trained Hamski to be mentally tough, to have personal and moral courage, to stand up for what he thought was right, and above all, to fight like hell for what he believed in. And that's precisely what he was going to do.

Captain Hamski refused to order his company to take the vaccine. He refused to pass down an order that was unethical. "I . . . believe . . . that commanders were breaking the law and putting service members' health in jeopardy," Hamski said. "My stance was and is that no service member should be forced to take any kind of medical intervention without informed consent, especially when the long-term effects of that medical procedure are not yet known. And if any attempt is made to force service members to receive a medical intervention, commanders take on a greater responsibility to dissent such an act in concern for the health and welfare of those they are charged with leading."

Some of his soldiers chose not to take the shot since Hamski wasn't ordering them to do so. This infuriated Hamski's commanders more than his own refusal. Since not all of the companies had given the order, that meant that the battalion commander had to issue a blanket order. The battalion commander ordered an "all hands" to the motor pool, the staging location for the unit's vehicles, which was frequently used as a meeting point for the large formation. The commander told the gathered battalion that if they were a "vaccine refusal," they had to step away from the rest of the group and enter into a side room. There the vaccine refusals were required to stand on one side of the room, and on the other side sat the battalion commander with his entourage: the battalion sergeant major, company commanders, the judge advocate general (military lawyer), and public affairs officer—a clear intimidation attempt. The battalion commander required everyone to watch a reeducation video from the CDC about the safety and efficacy of the vaccine. After the video, the battalion commander read the vaccine order for the second time.

As the only company commander on the refusal side of the room, Captain Hamski felt he had to stand up for that side of the room and say something. "This is not okay, sir," he began, "the vaccine is unproven. . . ." He started to say more, but was immediately cut off and silenced. The battalion commander dismissed everyone from the room. Captain Hamski later explained that the battalion commander's team viewed his and others' refusal as political, as though they were being conservatives who had bought into the COVID vaccine "misinformation," and that they were conspiracy theorists. Their legitimate health and welfare concerns were never considered.

A month later, in September, Captain Hamski was suspended from command and was told to clear out his office. His request to speak to

his soldiers about his absence was refused. A week later, he was officially relieved of his command and received a permanent GOMOR
(General Officer Memorandum of Reprimand), an automatic career
killer. Months later, in February 2022, Hamski received a "relief for
cause" officer evaluation report for his time as HHC commander, which
is another automatic career killer.

Hamski, a talented young officer with every qualification an
infantry officer could have and then some, was sad to see the military become as political as it has, especially in the officer corps.
He said there is grooming that starts when you're a lieutenant (the
lowest officer rank) that pushes you to make decisions with a political
mindset. Now, Hamski said he would not recommend service to young
Americans—not with the military's current status and politicized
leaders like General Milley. He has encouraged service members to
get out of the military when their contract is up until such time as the
Army can make itself whole again.

One of the hardest parts for Hamski was that the Army that he
loved, both as an institution and fighting force, threw him away. A
soldier with great potential and a clear pathway to rise within the ranks
had his career destroyed by senior officers influenced by time-serving
political hacks. He is just one of the thousands tossed aside with no
regard in a needless purge.

CHAPTER 5

Diversity Doesn't Actually Make Us Stronger

E Pluribus Unum: Out of Many, One

As a meritocracy, the military is already a diverse and inclusive organization. This didn't come about because administrators and commanders were tracking skin color, gender preference, sexuality, pronouns, origins, or class. The military took care of those differences at basic training and officer candidate school (OCS) by stripping everyone down to the same level, putting them in the same uniform, and putting an American flag patch on their right shoulder. Then came the process of rebuilding as a team, as warfighters in the United States military. Individuals' pasts no longer mattered, nor did it matter how they were raised, what color their skin was, if they were gay, what religion they followed, if their moms didn't like them or their fathers left when they were children. None of that was important now. Individuals were a part of an exclusive club that provided opportunity, direction, advancement, responsibility, and authority to people at very young ages. They shared a common bond with every American who has ever served. The military is uniquely able to give people of all backgrounds a clean slate.

After graduating from basic training or OCS, everyone starts in the same place, in the same rank. In the US military, a kid who grew up in inner-city Detroit on food stamps can rise through the ranks and become a general or a command sergeant major. How has the military been successful at this for decades? It focused on people's character, leadership, ability, devotion, and merit. Not on that person's past, his skin color, or his other differences.

But now President Biden and senior leaders at the Pentagon have turned away from meritocracy. Instead, high standards are being abandoned in the name of forced diversity, the fruitless quest for equivalent outcomes in all circumstances, and "inclusion." In time, this will destroy the military from the inside out.

In 2021, Secretary of Defense Lloyd Austin said, "The diversity of our nation makes us stronger. And that diversity in our military ranks makes us better at defending the American people."[1]

But does it really? Forced diversity for diversity's sake isn't what makes a military stronger. Instead, it divides the force. It means placing people in jobs because of their gender or skin color instead of assigning the best, most qualified person to the job. It means losing sight of the mission. It means lowering standards. It means quotas or target requirements instead of mission requirements. It causes resentment, breaches trust in leadership, and significantly damages morale.

Serving in the military is a dangerous job and not for the faint of heart. Service members need to be able to look to their left and their right and have full confidence in the ability of their team, to know that each team member is there because he is the best and most qualified person for the position.

The United States is the most diverse nation on this planet. Immigrants are successful, and they recognize the opportunities allotted to everyone regardless of background and differences. They take advantage of those opportunities to work for and achieve the American Dream. That's why people from around the world want to move here.

America is *already* a diverse nation. The military is no different. Diversity doesn't have to be forced or mandated. Concentrating on diversity instead of the mission is a recipe for disaster. We are seeing the implications of just such a strategy in the reduced standards, DEI training, and pressure not to take character and merit into account first when judging others. Plain and simple, this strategy is failing. The recruitment and retention numbers don't lie.

In 1963 Martin Luther King Jr. famously said, "I have a dream that my four little children will one day live in a nation where they will not be judged by the color of their skin but by the content of their character."[2]

He devoted his life to ensuring that people of different colors were treated equally. Equal opportunity, not equal outcomes. And he was absolutely right. There is no place in our society or the military for discrimination. We should live in a color-blind society where individuals are judged, hired, selected, and choose friends based on their character and who they are.

The Biden administration has taken the opposite stance from Martin Luther King Jr. and has decided that people's skin color *should* matter, as well as their gender and even their sexual orientation. That is how they want soldiers to be judged. On June 25, 2021, President Biden signed his Executive Order on Diversity, Equity and Inclusion and Accessibility in the Federal Workforce, stating, "The Federal Government should have a workforce that reflects the diversity of the American people."[3] The order prioritized DEI efforts and initiatives across the federal government. Biden gave all federal agencies one hundred days to determine "whether employees who are members of underserved communities face barriers to employment, promotion, or professional development within their workforce."[4] He also mandated that agencies create or elevate senior level positions known as chief diversity officers, whose sole priority is to promote and influence inclusion and diversity within federal organizations. The order made it mandatory for agency hiring processes to make all "gender markers and pronouns" available to respect nonbinary individuals, people who are non-gender conforming, and transgenders. They also have to start the process of moving towards gender-neutral facilities.[5]

Since the early days of the Biden administration, there has been an overt push for diversity in all aspects of the military: aviation, special operations, combat arms, and so on. These are the type of positions in which the nation should want the absolute best service members. Lives are at stake, and the success of our military and the success of our nation depend on these individuals. While the Obama administration made the initial steps towards a softer, more inclusive military, the Biden administration has taken the process to the extreme. The implication is that the military is weaker and less capable if every demographic, religion, sex, gender, creed, etc., is not represented or is under-represented in every unit across the military.

Diversity, equity, and inclusion is no longer encouraged, it's mandated. Units must have written strategies on how they are going to comply. Furthermore, there must be inclusion and representation for everyone, every type of uniqueness, however meaningless that difference might be for the task at hand.

The military cannot eliminate difficulties, whether they be with individual interactions or physical tasks. Facing adversity and difficulties is what makes people strong, mentally and physically. Hardships are essential for a warrior. Struggle makes you more capable. Pain makes you stronger. That's why Ranger school, Basic Underwater Demolition/ SEAL training, special forces selection, and other high-intensity courses push candidates to the limits of human ability. It is necessary to weed out mental and physical weakness. Only the strong succeed. Those struggles, hardships, and experiences unite. They bring the team together, helping everyone understand what others on the team went through to get there. This also mitigates operational risk on future missions. The military knows if it sends these elite soldiers into battle, they are much more likely to complete the mission, they are less likely to fail, less likely to quit. The military claims it is trying to pull from a larger talent pool—but it's actually diversity for the sake of diversity, and a recipe for unit weakness.

We have the best special operations force on the planet because our recruitment process is unmatched. Many people work for years to get selected into special operations units. It was designed to be hard. It was meant to be highly selective.

Unfortunately, in recent years, even Special Operations Command (SOCOM) hasn't been able to escape the wrath of the Pentagon's DEI obsession. In 2021, SOCOM released its Diversity and Inclusion Strategy, which begins with an apology: "We know that our force does not represent the diversity of our larger society—a fact that should give us pause. We have forms of bias that exist in our formation, making the journey of some of our teammates and family members a painful one."[6] That statement alone should give the entire nation pause. Why should our special operations leaders be concerned about how it "looks," or what the forces' gender preferences or sexual orientations are? 5.1 percent of Americans under thirty years old consider themselves transgender or nonbinary.[7] Are special operations leaders working towards ensuring that 5 percent of their fighting force is trans or nonbinary? I certainly hope not, but based on its DEI strategy, we may be getting there. But the world has not changed. There is no military mission whose success is determined by whether or not the force mirrors society's demographics. None.

The Pentagon needs to stop micromanaging and stop distracting from the mission with political agendas.

In the name of diversity and equity, military leaders claim that units are better if there are set percentages of people with certain types of skin color, ethnicities, sexual proclivities, and gender. This isn't about opportunity. This is about equity. But not every demographic from our society is qualified to serve in every occupation in the military. To do so means lowering standards instead of selecting the best man for the job, regardless of demographic information.

Defense Secretary Austin has said that "we're going to make sure that our military looks like America and that our leadership looks like what's in the ranks of the military."[8] How are they going to accomplish this? Quotas. Technically, quotas are illegal in military recruiting.[9] But there is a convenient work-around. At an Air Space and Cyber conference in 2020, the commander of the Air Force Recruiting Command, General Edward Thomas Jr., said when discussing the Air Force's new diversity recruiting goals, "This isn't a quota; it's a target."[10]

In 2022, the Air Force chief of staff and other Air Force leadership sent a memo to the force updating their officer demographics target goals. The memo said it is "imperative that the composition of our military services better reflect our nation's highly talented, diverse, and eligible population."[11] Their acceptable diversity target for officers commissioned into the Air Force and Space Force was: "67.5% white, 13% Black, 10% Asian, 7% multi-racial, 1.5% American Indian and 1% Native Hawaiian and Pacific Islander."[12] There was no mention of selecting the best people for the job regardless of skin color. That Air Force chief of staff, General Charles Q. Brown, was confirmed as the 22nd Chairman of the Joint Chiefs of Staff and General Milley's successor in September 2023.

"Diversity" for the sake of diversity divides the military. It divides people. It divides the team. It erodes trust. It creates resentment.

Equal opportunity means just that: the opportunity to try, not the opportunity to succeed. Nothing rips at the heart of unit morale like special treatment for a certain demographic of people over others. Soldiers are smart; they can easily see when a demographic gets special treatment. To its own peril, the military is focused on the individual now instead of the team. Equity has quickly replaced equality. Nothing more quickly erodes the team elements and standards that have made the US military the elite fighting force in the world.

In 2021 the Air Force unveiled a plan to make its pilot force more diverse. As of 2020, pilots in the Air Force were 88 percent white men.[13] In a DEI-focused world, that is now a problem. That's right: military leaders think aviation in the Air Force is too white. Now they are seeking minorities and women to become pilots, instead of allowing those of all backgrounds to apply if interested and then selecting the best candidate for the job. During an emergency, is any sane person going to say, "Thank God I had a mediocre pilot next to me, but at least she was a woman to meet unit diversity standards"?

In an interview with Defense One in March 2023, Marine Corps Commandant General David Berger was asked about the recent uproar from members of Congress and the American people surrounding the military focus on diversity training. He responded with, "I have seen zero evidence of any policies that detract from that. Everything—and I travel almost every week, mainly to listen, mainly to ask questions, not to talk but to listen. And I'm looking for anything that distracts them from their war fighting focus, what it takes to fight and win. I don't see any evidence of that."[14] But Berger had been at the Pentagon for too long, and he seemed to have forgotten that behind every general visit, the unit prepares for weeks to make sure the weeds are picked out of the grass, the offices are clean, and the books are in order. If the general does meet-and-greets or meals with soldiers, those soldiers are carefully selected and coached on how to act and what to say. It's a production.

Yet generals, who should know better, frequently think they're being presented with an honest snapshot of the troops.

On March 23, 2023, the House Military Personnel Subcommittee held a hearing to better understand how the diversity, equity, and inclusion effort was affecting warfighter readiness. One of the primary subjects was the matter of Kelisa Wing, a Pentagon official, who was hired by the Department of Defense in December 2021, as the Chief of Diversity, Equity and Inclusion of Department of Defense Education Activity (DoDEA), the military's education system that oversees 67,000 students and 159 schools around the world. Her position has a considerable amount of influence in DOD schools. DoDEA director Thomas Brady once praised Kelisa Wing as "exactly the right person to lead our efforts in building on the foundational work done to support meaningful change in our organization."[15] Then Wing came under fire in 2022 when several of her previous racist tweets came to light. In a July 2020 (and since deleted) tweet, she wrote:

> I'm so exhausted at these white folx in these PD [professional development] sessions this lady actually had the CAUdaacity to say that black people can be racist too . . . I had to stop the session and give Karen the BUSINESS . . . we are not the majority, we don't have power.[16]

When she used the word "CAUdaacity," she was referring to "caucasian audacity." She is also a contributor to a children's book called *What Is White Privilege? Racial Justice in America.* She has contributed to other children's books about defunding the police and Black Lives Matter.[17]

In September 2022, House Republican Representative Elise Stefanik sent a letter to the Department of Defense, demanding answers about Wing's racially divisive tweets. The Under Secretary of Defense for

Personnel and Readiness announced there would be a thirty-day review of Wing's actions. After not receiving a response, Congresswoman Stefanik sent a follow-up letter to Austin. Again, no response for six months from her initial inquiry. Then three hours prior to the subcommittee hearing on March 23, 2023, she got her reply from the Pentagon. The letter stated that Kelisa Wing had been transferred due to "headquarter restructuring." The new position she was placed in did not involve work with diversity, equity, and inclusion.[18]

Wing should have been fired. If the situation had been reversed, she *would* have been fired immediately for racism and not aligning with the values of the institution. The DOD knew exactly who it was hiring and had zero reservations about it. But Wing is a GS (general schedule) employee and therefore almost impossible to fire, even for a clearly justified offense. Instead, employees get "transferred." This way leaders are able to remove their current headache, but then in the process pass the problem on to someone else. This happens elsewhere in the military as well. When service members cause problems, leadership often transfers them to a new unit as someone else's problem, rather than dealing with the process and paperwork it will take to hold them accountable.

While at the Army's Associations annual conference in 2022, Secretary of the Army Christine Wormuth said, "I'm not sure what 'woke' means. I think woke means a lot of different things to different people."[19] She went on to deny that anything woke impacted the Army's war fighting ability or readiness. All is well from Wormuth's perspective, despite the Army facing the biggest recruitment crisis since the end of the Vietnam War.

How can an institution be expected to fix itself if its leaders refuse to acknowledge there is a problem?

Senior military leaders are taking a system that used to be based on standards and merit and throwing it away, replacing it with a system that points out everyone's differences and negative past experiences instead of focusing on what's important to the mission. Everyone in the military bleeds the same color. On the battlefield when the bullets are flying, no one cares what color you are, what gender you are, or what your sexual orientation is. They care about whether or not they can count on you to fight back, care for them if they get wounded, and work toward defeating the enemy.

Who benefits the most from a woke military? China, Russia, Iran, and the rest of our adversaries. China isn't spending millions of dollars on diversity training. China isn't wasting valuable training hours on DEI training. China isn't focused on restructuring its military infrastructure in order to appease society. China isn't focused on a green, battery-powered military fleet. China is focused on strategizing against the United States and training to defeat its woke military.

There's a simple way forward. The military must ditch the DEI woke culture and get back to focusing on what unites the force: the mission, cohesion, and patriotism. The military must get back to operating as a meritocracy, with equal opportunity for all, with people selected based on ability and merit, not physical features or individual uniqueness. That's the way the military has succeeded, and that's the only way for the military to remain as the strongest, most elite military in the world. Our nation's motto is E Pluribus Unum: Out of Many, One. Let's get back to it.

CHAPTER 6

Double Standards

"With equal opportunity comes equal responsibility."

Unknown

Since Barack Obama became president, there has been a push to fundamentally transform the military. Military leadership has become emboldened to bend the rules and ignore standards when necessary to push an agenda of equity and diversity. This agenda includes looking the other way for many women in special operations and a blatant double standard for women and transgender men during a wartime draft or national emergency—because women and transgender men don't have to register with selective service. Leaders have made decisions that have affected the entire force to its core, without considering the long-term effects.

Women have a long-standing history in the military and have made priceless contributions to our nation's defense and military. Being among the sisterhood of women who have served this country and worn the uniform is something the nearly two million female veterans take great pride in.[1] This is all the more reason why it is frustrating to see the advances women have made in the armed forces over the last few decades diminished by special treatment and double standards, in the hopes of making the fighting force more appealing to women for both recruitment and retention purposes.

Women belong in the military. Women can do most jobs in the military. Women have made exceptional contributions to our nation and have bravely fought and sacrificed. Women have in every way proven to be a valuable asset. So yes, women should have the equal opportunity to *pursue* career paths within the military that they are passionate about and are qualified for, but they must only be selected based on excellence, not equity. Lowering standards to remove barriers for women causes serious problems that affect everyone: the mission, morale, confidence, and camaraderie. These are all essential components to focus and operate as a successful team on the battlefield. But unfortunately, political agendas, quotas, equity, and the strive to get "firsts" have tarnished what so many trailblazing women in the military set out to accomplish: equal opportunity and fair treatment.

In December 2015, after a three-year study, then Secretary of Defense Ash Carter made a historic declaration that as of January 2016, women would be allowed to serve unrestricted in all combat jobs, including special operations. This included Navy Seals, Delta, Rangers, Infantry, and other grueling combat jobs. Prior to the announcement, the Department of Defense prohibited women from serving in 10 percent of military jobs, nearly 220,000 positions military wide.[2] Regardless, the DOD wanted to "make history" and seemingly catch up to the times in the civilian world. But are the stakes the same?

At face value, the seven guidelines for female integration released by the Department of Defense seemed to make sense:

1. Implementation will be pursued with the objective of improved force effectiveness.

2. Leaders must assign tasks and jobs throughout the force based on ability, not gender.

3. Equal opportunity likely will not mean equal participation by men and women in all specialties, and there will be no quotas.

4. Studies conducted by the services and Socom [Special Operations Command] indicate that on average there are physical and other differences between men and women, and implementation will take this into account.

5. The department will address the fact that some surveys suggest that some service members, men and women, will perceive that integration could damage combat effectiveness.

6. Particularly in the specialties that are newly open to women, survey data and the judgment of service leaders indicate that the performance of small teams is important.

7. The United States and some of its closest friends and allies are committed to having militaries that include men and women, but not all nations share this perspective.[3]

Doesn't it almost seem reasonable? No special treatment, no guarantees, no attempt to appease society. It essentially says men and women are different and that must be taken into account. It specifically says, "There will be no quotas."[4] Another good thing. It recognizes that jobs should be assigned based on ability, competence, and character, and that the best person should be selected for the job, regardless of gender. But like a lot of policies created at the top, when implemented in the ranks, this set of rules doesn't equate to the perfection it espouses on paper. Take rule five of the guidelines. It is an admission that there are legitimate concerns that the new policy could damage combat effectiveness. Their solution is to "trust the department"—they will "address" it. Before Ash Carter's decision, senior military and civilian leadership had studied the integration of women into combat positions. All branches and Special Operations Command had no exception requests, except for the Marine Corps.

The Marine Corps requested an exception for the infantry, machine gunners, fire support reconnaissance, and more. Essentially they were requesting to keep women out of combat jobs and keep them in support positions. General Joseph F. Dunford was the Marine Corps Commandant at the time, and he overruled the exception and made the decision to fully implement women into all Marine Corps jobs.

Implementation didn't quite go as planned. Once those restrictions were lifted, women didn't flood those positions the way officials thought they would. Once again, senior Pentagon leadership spent years of time, money, and efforts focusing on an issue that would drastically change the force, requirements, accommodations, and more, yet didn't benefit the military as a whole. It didn't make the military a stronger, more capable fighting force at all. Senior leadership was focused on optics rather than the litmus test of asking whether opening all combat jobs to women truly made the military more lethal.

Pentagon officials pushed countless man-hours onto commanders to enforce changes to policy and conduct sensitivity training. Military leaders focused on how female-friendly each unit was. Instead of commanders focusing on training that would help prepare Marines, Soldiers, Airmen, and Sailors to defeat the enemy in future conflicts, leadership prioritized time and training on women and how they could better accommodate them to appease political aims and military leadership's pet projects.

On paper or when briefing the press, Pentagon officials always stuck to the written rule: no special treatment, no quotas, no reduced standards. Yet if you read between the lines, the rules were steadily being bent. Instead of sticking to the clear guidelines the DOD initially released on how to integrate women into all positions in the military, commands started using the integration of women to their advantage.

There was the issue of "firsts." Many commanders wanted to be able to say their unit had the first female in the unit—it would be a great accomplishment for an officer to have on his employee review or officer evaluation report.

The US Army's Ranger School is the military premier tactical leadership school that tests students under stress and pressure in extreme environments. The school consists of Benning phase, Mountain phase, and the Swamp phase. Ranger students are sleep-deprived, food-deprived, and physically and mentally tested to their limits. The entire course is brutal. Only those with extreme mental and physical abilities succeed. About half of all men who start the course fail or quit.[5]

On August 21, 2015, two female officers graduated from Ranger School, one of the hardest leadership schools in the world, and in doing so made history by becoming the first women to graduate from the course. While Captain Kristen M. Geist and 1st Lieutenant Shaye L. Haver were awarded their Ranger Tab, they would not be allowed to command the type of combat arms job that most men hold after completion of Ranger School, like infantry, armor, or field artillery, until the ban was officially lifted four months later. Never one to miss a chance to make a political appearance, the future chairman of the Joint Chiefs of Staff, General Milley, was in attendance at the graduation.[6]

But after the graduation, the historic moment was overshadowed with accusations of special treatment, with the intent of having women graduate from Ranger School regardless of what standards had to be lowered or what rules had to be bent. One accusation was that General Scott Miller, who at the time was the commander of Maneuver Center of Excellence at Fort Benning, Georgia, performed undue command influence from the beginning to ensure a female would graduate. Multiple sources said that the general told a group of subordinates who were helping prep for the first-ever "gender-integrated assessment"—a special prep school to prepare women who were to attend Ranger School—that "a woman will graduate Ranger School. . . . At least one will get through."[7] Those statements sent a very clear message to the Ranger instructors who were normally tasked with ethically grading each candidate (who previously had only been men), to the standard, per the Ranger School's standard operating procedures policy, in an unbiased way. In January, months before the Ranger School start date of April 20, 2015, women were required to attend a two-week rigorous Ranger Training and Assessment Course (RTAC). This course is normally designed as a pre-Ranger assessment or prep school that helps individuals assess if they'll be able to handle Ranger School. It is usually a mandatory course for National Guard but was optional for active duty personnel. But all women who were selected to start Ranger School in April were required to attend and pass the course in January before being allowed to start the school on April 20. The issue was that men were held to a go/no-go standard. If the soldier got a no-go, he was out. There was no redo. But if the women in RTAC received a no-go, they were allowed to recycle the training and continue until they received a pass.[8]

The women who completed RTAC and progressed forward towards Ranger School then received more special treatment. They received nutrition counseling and lessons on how to conduct a ground patrol. They were even taken ahead of time to the actual land navigation course used during Ranger School to familiarize them with the course. The land navigation course is deemed one of the hardest parts of the course, and men are not allowed to see the course until they are in Ranger School and begin the tested part of the course. Women were paired with a Ranger who had completed the Army's Best Ranger Competition, one of the most grueling and difficult challenges in the military. His job was to prep the women candidates with everything they needed to know prior to starting Ranger School and give them an advantage on the course that the men didn't even have the luxury of glimpsing beforehand.[9]

Of the 140 women that attended RTAC in January, only nineteen started Ranger School on April 20, even with the significant special treatment and double standards for passing RTAC. Within a few days, eleven women left the course for injury, failures on the road march, failures during patrols, or other physical aspects. Only eight remained.[10]

After three weeks of Ranger School, on May 7, there were no women left. The eight that had made it to the Darby phase all failed by the end of this initial phase. General Scott Miller called those soldiers into a meeting. While the exact conversation remains unknown, General Miller confirmed in a statement that the meeting occurred and that he was impressed that eight women wanted to stay in the course and try to retest the phase they had failed. The next day, the eight women were allowed to recycle and redo the phase. By the end of May, five women were sent home. The remaining three failed their patrol evaluations. That's when allegations of undue command influence increased.[11]

Soon thereafter, General Miller went down to the Ranger training grounds and observed the area where the women were working on the course. Coincidentally, the three women remaining all passed their course after the general's visit.[12]

Eventually, two women passed the course and graduated on August 21, 2015.[13]

Speculation around special treatment had grown so significantly that General Miller felt the need to address the allegations at graduation, by sharing something that had been said at his own Ranger graduation years ago: "[The instructor] said, more or less, 'You have people who will question the standards of Ranger School. When they question those standards, what I ask you to do is invite them back to Fort Benning, Georgia, and re-validate their tab." Miller said that his instructor stated, "To date, we've had zero takers." Miller went on to proclaim, "Ladies and gentlemen, [Ranger Assessment Phase] week has not changed. Standards remain the same. . . . The five-mile run is still five miles. The 12-mile march is still 12 miles."[14]

But the problem wasn't that people were doubting if the distance was shorter for the women or men, or even if they were evaluated on a different time standard. The issue was that General Miller ensured that the women Ranger candidates were given an advantage no man received, and before the course even began, by the Army sending them through a mandatory training program, a test run of the land navigation course, and by granting multiple do-overs at RTAC. How many men throughout the course of Ranger school had a general officer invested in their individual success? None.

General Miller got his "first," and he got promoted and was given more responsibilities and opportunities. He went on to command JSOC—Joint Special Operations Command, the world's premier special operations unit—and was the top commander in Afghanistan just prior to the fall of Kabul in 2021. After retiring, he joined the board of directors of a defense contracting company that focuses on data analytics.

On October 7, 2015, Congressman Steve Russell of Oklahoma wrote a letter to the Secretary of the Army, John McHugh, due to concerning reports out of Fort Benning regarding the special treatment of women in Ranger School. When Russell spoke with an Army official, he was shocked to hear that the records he had requested to see from the Army had likely been destroyed. His letter stated, "I was somewhat puzzled by the Army officials informing me that many of the documents I am requesting might not be delivered as they may have been shredded."[15]

Tracks covered.

The Army has denied that any special treatment was given to women. Still, at a press conference following graduation, one of the women to graduate, Captain Kristen Geist, said, "I thought we were going to be dropped after we failed Darby [obstacle course] the second time. . . . We were offered a day-one recycle."[16]

Regardless of the extent of the special treatment and double standards, the fact that inconsistencies in standards between men and women exist at all severely damaged the trust service members had in the institution. Ranger School is one of the most respected and honored courses in the military. It has always set extremely high standards for a reason. The coveted black and gold Ranger Tab is something that is almost sacred in Army ground force units. It means that you are the best of the best. Everyone that wears the tab has a mutual understanding of the hardships they faced during the course and how they earned it. Everyone in the Army without a "tab" looks upon the Ranger-qualified soldiers with a certain level of respect and admiration, knowing they did something extremely difficult.

All of the speculation, accusations, and both positive and negative media attention shed light on the culture shift within the special operations community. Women were now expected to be there regardless of whether they'd earned it. That in and of itself weakens the credibility of the institution as a whole. It creates resentment. It changes the certainty that everyone who wears the tab earned it, no questions asked, such as: Did you earn the tab before or after women were allowed in? That's exactly why following standards is critical. Bending the rules for certain demographics to meet diversity goals is detrimental to morale and will bring the whole structure down.

It's not the fault of the women trying out. The first women to graduate Ranger School persevered through an incredible challenge and didn't ask for the political agenda behind their attendance. They went into these schools expecting fair and equal treatment, not special treatment and predetermined outcomes. It's the fault of leadership. It was they who veered from a high moral standard, placing the appearance of progression and inclusion in the ranks over substantive gains.

By 2021, five years after the ban on women in combat positions was lifted, it wasn't about equality anymore. It was about diversity and equity. Marine Corps Commandant General David Berger announced that more diversity was the answer to combat jobs, declaring that having enough women was now a requirement to get the job done.[17] Remember back not too long ago when the DOD put out guidelines specifically stating that women weren't necessarily right for every job, and selections should be individualized by skills, not gender? That didn't last very long. The Marine Corps went from requesting an exemption from the policy allowing women in combat jobs to announcing it can't accomplish *any* job without women.

When then Secretary of Defense Ash Carter lifted the ban on women in combat positions, they were given the opportunity to try. But that's not where it ended. The pendulum kept swinging. After women were serving in once-banned jobs, military leaders wanted even more women for representation and fairness. Now the directive was to recruit women and to make sure that women knew of specific job opportunities.

The harsh truth that the DOD fails to acknowledge is the fact that large numbers of women are *not* interested in combat arms jobs. The majority of women don't want to serve in combat arms. At all. Sure, some (very few) are interested in combat-oriented jobs, like being a helicopter pilot, or being in a female engagement team embedded with special operations forces, but even fewer are interested in the infantry. Most women that serve sign up for support positions like medical, mechanics, intel, cyber, legal, human resources, logistics, and so forth. Yes, sometimes those positions require convoys and other instances of being in harm's way. That is the nature of the modern military and the conflicts we've been involved in. But this is different than serving in the infantry or special operations. And that is fine.

Have women successfully and honorably served in specific combat arms and special operations jobs? Yes. There have been some incredibly brave female heroes. But that does not mean that every woman that joins the military should be in a combat or special operations unit. Just like not every man that joins the military should be in a combat or special operations unit. All that matters is that these types of units get the very best person for the mission. There should be a mission standard, not a gender standard. And that has nothing to do with the fact that a woman is more or less capable than a man. If those capable women want to, they should be given an opportunity to serve in the capacity that they want, but without special treatment. Without extra help or any other advantage not afforded to their fellow male service members.

However, it is not reasonable to expect or force military branches to overhaul their entire structure, culture, and model merely to accommodate a few women who wish to pursue combat arms jobs. Nor should they be expected to lower standards in an attempt to attract women to these positions merely to meet quotas or present their unit as "the most diverse." Commanders should not be allowed to use female percentages, "firsts," or accomplishments as an OER (officer evaluation report) bullet point to enhance their appearance and accomplishments on paper.

Furthermore, in the military context, diversity itself does not in fact improve our strength or capabilities to destroy the enemy. The priority should be to place the most ruthless, capable, and qualified people with the ability to succeed in the most demanding and challenging work environments. Gender quotas to appease the general public or to make the woke crowd feel good about women serving in the infantry should not be the military's concern. They should care about killing the enemy, destroying our adversaries, and winning wars. Not a lot of that going on right now.

In 2018 the Army made sweeping changes to its physical fitness test with the hope of the new test being a better assessment for combat success, while at the same time reducing injuries. It was the first of its kind in over forty years. The original fitness test consisted of three events: two minutes of push-ups, two minutes of sit-ups, followed by a two mile run. The first iteration of the new test expanded to six events including over throws, a run, planks, a sprint-drag-carry, leg tuck, deadlift, and push-ups. It involved balance, agility, flexibility, strength, speed, and more. The test was gender- and age-neutral—men and women took the same test.[18] The expectation was that regardless of your gender, you have to be able to complete the mission. Men and women fight the same enemy, so they should be required to pass the same physical test. Again, there should be a mission standard, not a gender standard.

Nearly half of women failed the test (44 percent) from October 2020 to April 2021. Only 7 percent of men failed the test. The Secretary of the Army raised concerns about the possibility that the new physical fitness test was damaging the Army's ability to retain women.[19] Basically, the concern was that higher fitness standards led to fewer women being interested in joining or staying in the military. The Army's response wasn't that only those who passed would be able to advance forward. Instead, the powers-that-be lowered the standard for women in order for them to pass the test. They "revised" the previous version of the test by eliminating certain events and changing the scoring scale. A female now only has to run two miles in twenty-three minutes and twenty-two seconds to pass the test. She only has to do ten hand release push-ups to pass.[20] Not exactly the level of fitness you would want of anyone, man or woman, serving in the finest army in the world.

Captain Kristen Geist, one of the first women to graduate from Army Ranger School, came out against lowering the physical standards for women, stating that the system would be harmful to the Army and women as a whole: "Under a gender-based system, women in combat arms have to fight every day to dispel the notion that their presence inherently weakens these previously all-male units. Lower female standards also reinforce the belief that women cannot perform the same job as men, therefore making it difficult for women to earn the trust and confidence of their teammates." She went on to say, "The presence of just a handful of individuals who cannot run two miles faster than twenty-one minutes has the potential to derail a training exercise, not to mention an actual combat patrol." She continued, "Missions will be delayed and other soldiers will be overburdened with the weight of their unfit teammates' equipment. This scenario is inconvenient and bad for morale during a training exercise; in combat it could be deadly."[21]

Physical fitness is held to a high standard in the military. It's a common assumption that if you are physically fit and score well on your test, you're probably good at most everything else having to do with your job. It means you care about leading by example. It earns people's respect.

There must be a standardized military branch fitness test. Additionally, there needs to be Military Occupational Specialty (MOS)–specific testing for certain jobs that are gender- and age-neutral. But ignoring the reality of the effects of a lowered standard test is another failure of military leadership. When standards are lowered in the military, someone else ends up carrying the weight. Another member of the team has to do more, especially in ground combat roles. This damages morale, hurts unit cohesion, and ultimately weakens the force. It hurts women, it hurts the unit, it hurts the military.

Another reason why physical fitness standards are so important in the military culture is that when everyone is held to the same standard, unit cohesion is born. Everyone knows they have been through the same level of suck. But that bond is broken once people arrive at that unit because of forced equity. Once people realize that an individual was held to a different standard, that individual will be an outsider, regardless of who he or she is or how he or she looks. And then the complaints of unfair treatment will begin; they will divide the unit and result in the breakdown of what is essential for mission success: team trust and morale. The brotherhood that you so often hear about in military culture, especially in the special operations community, isn't a made-up Hollywood fantasy. It is something that is earned and developed after everyone goes through the same hardships and sacrifices and brutal training. That is what unites everyone and makes the team whole. Take that esprit de corps away because of woke agendas and special treatment, and you're in for a world of hurt.

In recent years there have been lots of "firsts" for women in the military, but how about the first women being required to register for the selective service in the name of equality?

All men in the United States must register for the selective service within thirty days of their eighteenth birthday, although they are given a window through their twenty-sixth birthday.[22] Today, women still do not have to sign up for the selective service. In January 2016, the Pentagon removed any and all barriers preventing women from serving in combat roles in the military. They are eligible to be assessed for every job. A military draft is intended to fill combat positions during a time of war or national emergency if the all-volunteer force is unable to sustain itself. Combat jobs used to only be available for men, hence an all-male military draft. But now that women are serving in combat roles, an all-male draft is discriminatory and perhaps unconstitutional towards *men*. Of course women cannot perform the same way as men in infantry type combat jobs. Biologically it isn't possible. The selective service and

Congress know this, which is why they haven't updated the law to reflect this gender-neutral society we live in. To do so would prove disastrous.

Yet in 2019 a federal judge in Texas ruled that an all-male draft is unconstitutional. The plaintiff argued that the male-only requirement violated their Fifth Amendment due process clause in the Constitution as well as violating the equal protection clause. Previous justification for a male-only draft was that only men could serve in combat roles. Additionally, the judge weighed in on female capabilities in combat: "The average woman could conceivably be better suited physically for some of today's combat positions than the average man, depending on which skills the position required. Combat roles no longer uniformly require sheer size or muscle."[23] But the Pentagon already made that decision unilaterally in 2016 when it lifted the ban. The decision now is whether a male-only selective service registration is discriminatory toward men.

In 2017, in a report to Congress, the Pentagon sided with requiring women to register for the selective service: "It would appear imprudent to exclude approximately 50 percent of the population—the female half—from availability for the draft in the case of a national emergency. . . . And, if a draft becomes necessary, the public must see that it is fair and equitable. For that to happen, the maximum number of eligible persons must be registered."[24] Prior to leaving office, President Obama, whose Pentagon has previously overturned the ban on women in combat jobs, supported a universal draft.[25]

In March 2020, the National Commission on Military, National, and Public Service released its report recommending that the draft remain in order to "maintain a military draft mechanism in the event of national emergencies. To meet military personnel needs in the face of future threats and to demonstrate America's resolve to international allies and adversaries, the Nation needs the Selective Service System to remain a viable national security institution." The report also recommended that registration be expanded to women as a "necessary and fair step."[26] Nevertheless, women are still not allowed to register for selective service.

Allowing women to serve in the military in all capacities is popular with the American public right now. Requiring women to register for the selective service is not. So because of political popularity, the double standard remains, and they get to have it both ways. It's a two-tiered system.

As an additional hypocrisy, the selective service system's stance on transgenders is problematic, not to mention discriminatory. Transgender men (that is, women) are not required to register for the selective service. Transgender women (that is, men) are required to register for selective service. This is because the selective service says that "sex at birth" must match registration.[27] So the selective service is allowed to acknowledge a person's actual, true sex, but the people in the military are required to play to people's gender preferences and identities. In fact, as I'll discuss shortly, the taxpayer is on the hook for paying for their gender affirming health care and special treatment.

The double standards and special treatment that are prevalent in the military today will do tremendous damage to our nation. They will make the fighting force weaker, more resentful, and more divisive than ever. They will destroy the military. This has already started.

CHAPTER 7

Military Pride

"Appeasement only makes the aggressor more aggressive."
Dean Rusk

The military is actively trying to divide people and focus on soldiers' differences rather than being an organization that brings people together, regardless of those differences. The irony is that the military claims it is acting in the name of "inclusiveness"; however, the actions and decisions from our military's senior leaders are designed to create dividing lines. Those who join the service have always come from different backgrounds, but those differences didn't matter. Once you got through basic training, you were a Soldier, Sailor, Airman, or Marine, and no one cared about your background. The military is the great equalizer. It does not matter if you grew up in a rich neighborhood or a poor neighborhood, or if you were a Black guy or a white girl. What mattered was if you could hold your own and help take care of those to your left and right when they needed help. What counted was if you were a liability or an asset. Race, gender, sexual orientation, and other qualities did not come into the equation; all that mattered was whether you could do your job and do it well. And even if you weren't that great at your job, if you still tried, improved, and continued to serve, then you were part of a sacred brotherhood and sisterhood. Your real identity was written on a tag over your left breast pocket on your uniform: US Army, US Marines, US Navy, US Air Force, or US Space Force. Now the military wants people to focus on their unique differences instead of being part of a cohesive unit that is able to look past differences and work together to accomplish the mission. Erasing individual genders is absurd and a bizarre attempt to appease a very small percentage of the population. Five percent of Americans under thirty consider themselves to be nonbinary or transgender.[1]

The military now celebrates Pride month in June as an official recognition month. The rainbow flag is splattered across social media posts for the month to show just how much the military supports a community that has a different sexual preference than almost all of them. As part of that recognition, bases across the country host drag shows that are referred to as "family friendly," in the name of inclusion and diversity. Some of these have even been catered specifically towards children at military base libraries. This type of "inclusion" shows weak leadership, appeasement, and the non-seriousness of our military. These burlesque-style shows are hyper-sexualized. They don't belong on a military base, they don't belong at a family event, and they certainly don't belong anywhere near children.

An Air Force leadership group is requiring airmen to use non-gender specific pronouns when writing award citations. They are now instructed to use gender-neutral pronouns. Instead of he/she/his/her, they are supposed to use Airman, Member, Individual or "they."[2] The Air Force also officially updated its writing guide and now allows airmen and guardians to use their pronouns in email signature blocks, as well as official memorandums and documents with male, female, or X.[3] All of this in the name of being more inclusive. In 2020, the Air Force chief of staff ordered the lyrics of the Air Force song be updated in order to include women. The song has not been changed for eighty years.[4]

Navy SEALS changed their ethos and creed to remove "brotherhood" and "men." The second-to-last section now reads, "Brave SEALs," instead of "Brave men."[5] Although women are allowed to try out for Navy SEAL teams, there are currently no women who have actually become a Navy SEAL. The Navy put out a training video featuring Navy engineers, dressed in rainbow-colored clothing, discussing the importance of affirming someone's gender preference by using their proper pronouns and actions to take if sailors are unsure what to do in those situations.[6]

The Army released woke cartoon recruiting ads that showed a lesbian couple attending an LGBTQ+ rally/march and a lesbian wedding. The soldier described her childhood as "normal," growing up with two moms and fighting for equality. She later went on to say that she joined the military to help the military shatter stereotypes.[7] That's promoting activism, not patriotic service.

The ads were clearly created to reach a very specific and tiny demographic of the American population. Military recruiting ads that focus on courage, war fighting, camaraderie, and the adventurous nature of the military are what sell. And these qualities are what attract the type of people who believe in our nation and what it stands for to fight in its defense. But again, the military has shifted from ads that spark patriotic fire in young people and highlight cool jobs with intense responsibilities and has replaced them with woke ads, targeted toward identity group appeasement and qualities that have nothing to do with the military or defending our nation.

Enemy soldiers don't care if you grew up with two moms, or two dads, or a mom and a dad, when they shoot you. They care that you are an American, and to them an American soldier represents everything they want to destroy.

Where does this end? What do the firsts, the shattering stereotypes, the mandated inclusiveness and acknowledgment of every single difference out there, get for us *militarily*? What possible authentic mission could they serve? And where does the military's willingness to bend over backwards to appease those requests end? What does it cost in time and treasure?

As of now, it doesn't end, and the system is breaking down as a result.

In July 2022, Joint Base Langley-Eustis held a drag show at its Diversity, Equity, and Inclusion summer festival. It was advertised as kid-friendly, and as an addition to a drag show the base included standard kid attractions, including a "bouncy house and face painting." The event was held on base and was paid for with military funding—meaning the tax dollars of honest and hard-working Americans. The drag performer, Joshua Kelley, also known as Harpy Daniels, joined the Navy in 2016.[8] Perhaps as a way to fund his drag hobby? A top military official signed off on the approval for the event.[9]

During Pride Month in 2022, Ramstein Air Force Base planned a thirty-minute drag queen story hour for military children at the library on the base, with a drag queen named Stacy Teed. Ramstein, home to the largest air base in Germany, wised up and canceled the show. According to the chief of public affairs at Ramstein, the drag show was not properly vetted, nor had it gone through the appropriate channels for approval. Nevertheless, the spokesperson felt the need to add, "Ramstein leaders strive to foster a culture based on inclusion where all people are treated with dignity and respect, regardless of their political views, color of their skin or sexual orientation."[10]

The year before, in June 2021, Nellis Air Force Base, known as "home of the fighter pilot" in Las Vegas, Nevada, took part in the disturbing trend. The Air Force base has a "Pride" committee that planned the event called Drag-U-Nellis. The base said the event was to boost morale and facilitate inclusivity and diversity. It featured multiple drag queens from Las Vegas. The military show's flier said that the drag show would help military families "discover the significance of drag in the LGBT+ community." A statement provided to Newsweek by Nellis Air Force Base said, "Nellis Air Force Base is committed to providing and championing an environment that is characterized by equal opportunity, diversity and inclusion. Base leaders remain supportive of events and initiatives that reinforce the Air Force's emphasis on diversity and inclusion toward recognizing the value every one of our Airmen brings to the team."[11] Nellis is home to the US Air Force Warfare Center, whose mission is advanced combat aviation training.

It is absolutely bizarre that military commanders are approving drag shows on their military bases. The military used to have a strict professional standard. But now, it seems, if anything is promoted under "honoring diversity and inclusion," it's something that has the new military command's full support. Good order and discipline are staples of the military. Military leaders pride themselves on the fact that they are held to a higher standard. Allowing drag shows on base demonstrates a level of non-seriousness as a professional organization and a waste of taxpayer dollars and use of facilities. It also makes some families on base feel quite uncomfortable and excluded from the once tight, respectful, dignified, and professional military community.

But if we're going to have drag, why the double standard? Men are allowed to dress up and mock women in sexual costumes and parade around a military event, on a military base, in the name of Pride and diversity and inclusion. Are female strippers allowed on military bases to do shows during Women's History month in the name of women's empowerment? Why not? Is it because strippers would cause issues that could be perceived as unprofessional, detract from readiness and the mission, cause issues within the marriages, and possibly even—gasp, make families feel excluded? Drag shows do the exact same thing, but level-headed, common-sense people who oppose them have been forced into silence out of fear of retaliation, of being called a bigot, and of being canceled.

The fact that this has been allowed and continues to be normalized is absurd and embarrassing for the institution as a whole. It really must stop. The military has lost significant trust with the American people. When people hear the military has the time, effort, and money to sanction and pay for drag shows, people stop viewing it as a serious organization. Serving in the military is an honor and a privilege. Drag shows paint the institution as an unserious joke.

On March 30, 2023, at a House Armed Services Committee hearing, Representative Matt Gaetz asked Secretary Austin why drag shows were taking place on military bases around the world and why they were supported by the Department of Defense. The defense secretary attempted to deny that they happen at all or that DOD supports them, despite the evidence that the congressman presented, including four separate instances of scheduled drag shows on military bases. General Milley later interjected that he would like to see the fliers for those drag shows and that he disagrees with their being scheduled.[12] Secretary Austin could end this nonsense in an instant. He required the entire military to get the COVID vaccine. He could just as easily write a memo to every DOD installation across the globe prohibiting drag shows or the like from ever being held on a military base again.

It says a lot about the culture that has been fostered that bases and their commanders feel comfortable sanctioning these drag shows on military installations. And if they don't feel comfortable, they likely feel cowed by the wrath they will face by LGBTQ+ activists if they don't. The only one so far who has been brave enough to cancel was the commander at Ramstein Air Base. Bold, decisive leaders are not rewarded at the moment, and the senior leaders that remain clearly lack the backbone to stand up to the woke mob and make the common sense decision to ban drag shows from their military bases.

In January 2021, about eight months prior to the fall of Afghanistan, the Army released its updated policy for grooming and appearance standards. The Army now allows male soldiers to wear clear nail polish while in uniform. The Army claims this is in an effort to increase the wellbeing of soldiers. Sergeant Major Brian Sanders, the senior enlisted leader of Army G-1's uniform policy branch, said, "This is one of the many facets of putting our people first and recognizing who they are as human beings. . . . Their identity and diverse backgrounds are what makes the Army an ultimate fighting force."[13]

Allowing men to wear nail polish doesn't make them stronger, more lethal fighters on the battlefield. But it does make a few feel more comfortable, and that's where the military's focus is these days. The Army also removed wording in the previous grooming policy which was said to be "offensive and weaponized," such as: "Mohawk, Fu Manchu, dreadlock, eccentric, and faddish."[14] It is truly hard to keep up with what is offensive these days.

Serving in the military isn't about one individual's feelings. In fact, it's not about the individual at all. It's about serving something greater than yourself. It's about protecting our nation's way of life and upholding our liberties and values. And the way to do that is for individuals to selflessly put unique characteristics to the side, become a part of a team, and do what's best for that team. Highlighting individual identity instead of teamwork, giving certain demographics special treatment—that is how you kill morale. And this is especially hard on young leaders, captains, responsible for young troops who joined the military to serve and to be a part of something great. Captains know those under them are looking to their company commanders to support them and do the right thing. Instead, these commanders spend huge amounts of time explaining their way out of common sense.

The military is trying to appease an unappeasable demographic. Our military's leaders need to stop pandering to social constructs that ebb and flow with the current trends. The military is not supposed to be trendy. The military is not a social club. Its job is not to make you feel good about yourself, or make you feel pretty, or validate your every insecurity. It is supposed to uphold rigid professional and grooming standards that those who are serving must adhere to. Why? Because good order and discipline breed effectiveness. It's about training you to be the most lethal warfighter in the world to fight our nation's enemies. Want to earn your spot at the table? Work hard. Earn your place on the team. Do those things you don't necessarily want to do every day, like waking up at 5:00 a.m. to go running and do push-ups, but do it anyway because it builds character and because people are counting on you to be the best version of yourself. Adhering to standards makes you mentally tough. Doing hard things every day makes you even tougher. It gives you discipline. It teaches you that some things are bigger than you and how you currently prefer to style your hair or paint your nails.

World War II veterans would be ashamed knowing that military standards have slipped so far. We now have a military where men are allowed to wear nail polish and might draw back in offended horror if someone uses the word "mohawk" to describe a haircut. The military used to be hard. It used to be tough. It used to be made up of warriors who had better things to do than worry if they could wear nail polish in uniform. And you know what some of those warriors shaved on to their heads prior to jumping out of an aircraft behind enemy lines? A mohawk. A kinder, gentler military will not yield the results its leaders are hoping for. This isn't summer camp, where we are all sitting around a campfire singing together. This is the military, where we are supposed to be protecting our nation's way of life by violently taking the lives of enemies.

It is pretty simple: if something doesn't make the military a stronger, more vicious fighting force, then it shouldn't be a priority.

On June 30, 2016, President Obama's defense secretary, Ash Carter, announced that the Pentagon had lifted the ban on transgender troops in the military. Transgenders could serve openly and without limitations and could no longer be kicked out or discharged solely for being transgender. The new policy also called for transgenders to be allowed to enlist in the military starting in 2017. This is an important note, because usually the military is more lenient with conditions discovered once someone is already serving. If those conditions are present prior to enlisting, that person may be disqualified because of the condition or may be required to pursue a waiver.[15] Secretary Carter cited a study (that he had ordered) and three primary reasons for lifting the ban: "the force of the future, the existing force and matters of principle."[16] But clearly, the decision was political. The DOD announced it almost at the end of Obama's second term and knew it would take over a year to implement.

In Secretary Carter's brief to the defense press corps at the Pentagon announcing the change in policy, he said the "Defense Department must have access to 100 percent of America's population for its all-volunteer force to be able to recruit from among the most highly qualified, and to retain them."[17] The problem with this statement is that the Department of Defense has never had access to 100 percent of the population; it hasn't even come close for decades due to factors such as obesity and mental and physical health issues.

So was lifting the ban on transgenders really about equality, or was it about the DOD's inability to recruit in a younger population that accepts transgenders and gender fluidity? Or was the DOD really just worried about its reputation? Had its recruiting numbers gotten so dismal that it was now having to cater to a minuscule but expensive demographic? Did allowing transgenders to serve make the military a stronger fighting force more capable to destroy our adversaries, or was it a distraction from that mission?

The issue is not about the individual. It's about accommodating the few while ostracizing the majority. It's about losing track of mission priorities. It's about men dressing up as women, sharing showers with females, and the fear that comes with that for many women. It's about making others suffer so one individual, maybe two, in a unit can be catered to. It's about how the Department of Defense doesn't want to reshuffle infrastructure and create new transgender bathrooms and locker rooms—instead the DOD will just make women shower with men, if those men claim to be women, and force a trend on people who don't believe in it.

At the same time that the military is trying to include transgenders, they are isolating, excluding, and preventing individuals with certain religious beliefs from exercising freedom of religion. Service members with certain religious objections feel as though their religious freedoms have been disregarded in the name of making others feel included. Several service members I interviewed on the issue spoke in a low voice when talking about transgenders they are serving with, certain they might be in for trouble by calling a man a man—especially when that man went on leave for three months and came back cut to pieces and dressed as a woman. Many felt they were expected to provide encouragement or applaud individuals who transitioned. But many people are appalled. Most people also don't feel it is their responsibility to call someone by hokey pronouns. Most people live in reality, where there are only two genders. But the military is reeducating the force on pronouns and gender preference inclusivity despite the fact that a large majority of silenced individuals don't believe that they should have to relearn the English language and acknowledge an obvious lie. Some military branches are even threatening service members if they purposely "misgender" trans persons—meaning to call them by the wrong pronouns.[18]

This is a surefire way to destroy trust and unit cohesion. Moreover, any good Army recruiter knows he often must convince the parents of the recruits as much as the recruits themselves. Now parents of potential female army recruits must worry that their daughter will be forced to shower during basic training with men who decided to identify as women. The military is constantly trying to increase the number of women in the force to increase diversity quotients, yet this policy is counter to recruiting those women.

In December 2022, a Maru/Blue poll found that 80 percent of the service members felt that the recent change in policy that now allows transgenders to serve openly in the force caused "a great deal/some" to decrease their trust in the military.[19] That impact will have lasting consequences for the force. A military whose force doesn't trust its leaders or its policies will not survive.

Between 2016 and 2021, the US military spent roughly $15 million on transgender troops for gender affirming care–related issues, including $11.5 million on psychotherapy and $3.1 million on "gender reassignment surgeries" including removing testicles and breasts, labiaplasties, and hysterectomies. Six hundred and forty service members received hormone therapy, to the tune of $340,000.[20] As of 2021, around 2,200 transgenders in the military had been diagnosed with gender dysphoria or were seeking medical treatment such as hormone therapy and or surgeries.[21] Gender dysphoria is "psychological distress that results from an incongruence between one's sex assigned at birth and one's gender identity."[22]

The military is now required to provide medical specific treatment for transgender individuals as well as "transition" care. Those individuals are also able to serve openly in their identified gender, differing from their true sex. Additionally, the military is required to provide full access to all gender-specific facilities, including bathrooms and showers. Men—men with penises, male bodies, and all that entails, yet who claim to "identify" as women—are allowed full use of women's showers. So if your daughter wants to serve her country out of a sense of patriotic duty and is in the same unit as a man who decided he wanted to present as a woman, your daughter could be forced to shower next to that man—who may or may not be leering at her. Do you think that would make her feel included? What would that do to her morale, her readiness? What about her fellow women in the unit? How many of them would be scared, intimidated, and mentally distracted from doing their job and accomplishing their mission because they knew, at the end of the day, they'd have to use the same shower as a man who could stand there watching them bathe?

Upon lifting the ban, Secretary Carter said, "This is the right thing to do for our people and for the force. . . . We're talking about talented Americans who are serving with distinction or who want the opportunity to serve. We can't allow barriers unrelated to a person's qualifications [to] prevent us from recruiting and retaining those who can best accomplish the mission."[23]

But those barriers *are* related to an individual's qualifications. Serving in the military is not available to everyone. There are plenty of talented Americans who want to serve their country, who would otherwise be qualified without running into barriers that the military has in place, but can't because the military lists certain conditions as unqualified. No one has the right to serve in the military. The military should be exclusive. A 2020 Pentagon study found that 77 percent of Americans would not be eligible for military service because of obesity, drug use, and other mental and physical health problems. That's up 6 percent since 2017.[24]

But why the double standard? Why is the military willing to bend over backwards to allow individuals with a claimed medical condition like gender dysphoria, previously deemed disqualifying, to receive special accommodations and expensive medical and psychological treatments, leading to a medical profile that prevents them from deploying, sometimes for years? Individuals with asthma after the age of thirteen are disqualified from serving in the military and service academies. Military services may consider a waiver on a case-by-case basis, but only when it has been determined that the asthmatic condition no longer exists: "Waivers may be possible, but only if convincing evidence suggests that a diagnosis was erroneous or that the condition has credibly resolved. Ongoing use of medication to treat or prevent bronchospasm does not convey resolution of such a condition and will result in waiver denial."[25] Surely there are jobs that someone with asthma could do. They could work in HR, they could work in the medical field, or they could be a cook. There are many support (non-combat) jobs in the military. People with asthma work in those fields in the civilian sector. Why is the military picking and choosing who gets special treatment and accommodations? Why are transgenders afforded more special treatment than people with asthma or other conditions? Those individuals didn't choose to be asthmatics, yet many of them still want to serve.

And if the Secretary of Defense continues to push the narrative that people's medical conditions shouldn't prevent them from patriotic service from the military, then why are those individuals excluded? There is no social movement in our nation right now in favor of people with asthma. In fact, most people probably find it reasonable that people with asthma aren't allowed to serve because of their condition.

If a teenager receives an anxiety diagnosis after the loss of a loved one, or during his or her parents' divorce, and is prescribed anxiety medication for it, he or she, too, could be disqualified from service. But transgenders are allowed to serve with no restrictions, including use of their preferred-gender bathroom. Other people disqualified from serving are those with orthodontic braces—they are disqualified from joining the military while they have braces; they can enter the delayed entry program, and once the braces come off they can start their training. Food allergies like a peanut or gluten allergy are also disqualifying conditions. So are skin conditions like eczema and psoriasis.[26] While waivers exist for some of these disqualifying conditions, most require a medical professional to prove that the condition no longer exists. If they are unable to prove it, the waiver will be denied. What it comes down to is, all of these conditions require special accommodations and medical care. They would require the military to have to drastically change things in order to allow these people to serve in the military and would hence take time, focus, and effort away from training and readiness and, overall, the mission.

The Obama administration didn't seem to think through the consequences of its drastic social engineering within the military. When it lifted the ban on women and allowed women to serve in combat positions, the brass guaranteed the country that standards would not change and they would maintain a merit-based, not quota-based, system. Similarly, with the transgender policy, the DOD rushed to get the historic ban lifted before Obama left office, without thinking of how implementation would actually work and how it would affect readiness of the force. Moreover, this new policy never considered the impact on the vast majority of the force that did not have gender dysphoria. The policy never considered how extreme appeasement of the few would completely alienate the majority.

In 2017, President Trump tweeted that he intended to reverse the Obama decision to lift the ban and prohibited transgenders from serving. In multiple tweets, the president said, "After consultation with my Generals and military experts, please be advised that the United States Government will not accept or allow . . . Transgender individuals to serve in any capacity in the US Military. Our military must be focused on decisive and overwhelming . . . victory and cannot be burdened with the tremendous medical costs and disruption that transgender [*sic*] in the military would entail."[27]

The following year the plan was enacted by Secretary of Defense Jim Mattis in 2018. Transgenders already serving were able to remain as long as they served in their biological gender. If they had gender dysphoria and they received an exception, they could serve in their biological sex. For those looking to enlist, transgenders with gender dysphoria were banned, unless they were stable for thirty-six months and willing to serve in the capacity of their true sex. If they had been on cross-hormone therapy or had sex reassignment surgery, they were disqualified.[28] Fast forward years later, and you find that those who didn't want to take the COVID-19 emergency-authorization vaccine were forced out—they didn't get the "grandfathered in" treatment like transgenders who were current service members under that policy change.

In March 2019, the Department of Defense put out a fact sheet on transgender policy that stated:

> To maintain a military force that is worldwide deployable and combat effective, the military must set high standards, and all military members must sacrifice to meet these standards. In fact, just over 70 percent of prime military-age Americans cannot meet the military's standards.
>
> Anyone who meets military standards without special accommodations can and should be able to serve—this includes transgender persons. Persons with a history of gender dysphoria—a serious medical condition—and who have undergone certain medical treatment for gender dysphoria, such as cross-sex hormone therapy or sex reassignment surgery, or are unwilling or unable to meet the standards associated with their biological sex, could adversely impact unit readiness and combat effectiveness.

For this reason, such persons are presumptively disqualified
for service without a waiver.[29]

Multiple lawsuits followed, but the Supreme Court upheld the
policy. Yet transgenderism is now a protected class under woke
ideology.

Once President Biden took office in January 2021, he quickly
reversed Trump's transgender ban. The administration continued pro-
mulgating the false notion that transgenders make the military stronger.
A press release during March 2022 said, "Transgender people are some
of the bravest people in our nation."[30]

It is also important to understand that active duty military service
members who opt for cosmetic surgery follow specific rules when it
comes to their medical procedure. First, elective cosmetic surgery,
such as breast augmentation or a nose job, must be approved by the
unit commander prior to surgery. Second, cosmetic surgery requires a
service member to take his or her own personal leave, not convalescent
leave, or leave that is granted to the service member without charge
(which is normally afforded to service members after a surgery required
after an accident). And finally, for normal elective cosmetic surgery,
the service member must pay for the procedure out of his or her own
pocket—the benefits of the 100-percent medical coverage that comes
with military service does not apply to elective cosmetic procedures.[31]

Why? Readiness. In order to be trained and ready to fight and
defend our nation, our military must devote its time and resources
toward readiness. Elective cosmetic surgery is permitted in the military
with certain stipulations. If service members want particular cosmetic
procedures, they are free to pursue them, but they just must do so on
their own time and on their own dime.

But there's also the greater point of appropriateness, civility, and
knowing the difference between right and wrong. The DODs states

that, "With regard to facilities subject to regulation by the military, a Service member whose gender marker has been changed in DEERS [the military-wide Defense Enrollment Eligibility Reporting System] will use those berthing, bathroom, and shower facilities associated with his or her gender marker in DEERS."[32] Women who sign up to serve in the military should not be subjugated to keeping company with naked men, regardless of the gender they identify as, especially in women's locker rooms, showers, and bathroom spaces. And vice versa with men. Women should have the right to feel safe and comfortable when getting ready for work after working out. And it will be women who lose out. They will shift their schedules, go to work late, have their professional reputation tarnished, etc., because many will wait until the transgender person leaves the facilities. Once again, others will have to rearrange their lives to accommodate transgenders and people with gender dysphoria.

President Trump's decision to ban transgender service was fairly straightforward. He rightly didn't think that transgender service members made the US military a stronger fighting force. Military service is bigger than one individual person. The military is not supposed to emulate woke universities that indoctrinate young Americans and turn them into activists. The military is supposed to be a disciplined and focused and cohesive unit that concentrates on the betterment of the team, not primarily on the individual soldier.

When General Milley went to the White House and interviewed with President Trump to be the next chairman of the Joint Chiefs of Staff, Trump asked Milley about his stance on transgenders, stating that Secretary of Defense Mattis implied that Milley might be weak on the transgender issue. Milley replied that he wasn't weak on transgenders; he said he doesn't care about who sleeps with who.[33] That's a righteous, dumb answer meant to shut down the conversation rather than discuss the real problems transgenders bring that make the military a less effective, lethal fighting force. That's an old talking point from the "don't ask, don't tell" days. But Milley's response shows that he doesn't care or understand what impact the implications of special treatment towards transgenders have on the force, or how they affect soldiers and the overall readiness of the military. The transgender issue has nothing to do with "who's sleeping with who," and that response clearly shows lack of judgment and understanding of the concerns around the issue. Transgenders are electing to be taken out of the fight, and service members with serious mental and behavioral issues are afforded special treatment and accommodation. Subordinates see this ridiculousness and lose trust in their leaders. Military leadership uses the readiness factor for almost everything, and then completely ignores its own requirement when it comes to transgenders removing themselves from the fighting force for months or years for transition surgery and treatment—and always at the taxpayers' expense. What is going to happen when one of our adversaries refers to someone in our military with the wrong pronoun? Are service members now so sensitive that they won't be able to fight that day, as they try to find someone to complain to because they feel disrespected? If so, they are likely to be killed or rolled over by a laughing enemy.

The military preaches standards and fairness, but the institution has failed to acknowledge how these transgender policies are damaging morale and retention. Gender dysphoria distracts from the mission and national security. Just as it was banned prior to 2016, gender dysphoria should be a disqualifying condition due to the instability surrounding it that contributes to the reduced effectiveness and readiness of the force. People with certain mood disorders or asthma are disqualified from serving. It's not because the military doesn't like people who are experiencing a mental health issue or because it wants to discriminate against them; it's because of the effects they have on the mission and readiness.

Transgenders pose another risk to the force. Transgenders attempt suicide eight times more than the rest of the US population.[34] Additionally, transgenders incur significantly higher medical costs. Many advocates for transgenders in the military point to the fact that the tens of millions of dollars that are spent on transgender physical and mental health care, hormone therapy, and surgeries are a mere drop in the bucket to the military's annual health care. Yet making the argument that tens of millions of dollars is nothing when it comes to the massive defense budget feeds into the already negative impression most Americans have of the Pentagon's wasteful spending.

Moreover, it is impossible to account for the amount of time lost due to the DOD's transgender policy. How much time was spent training commanders and soldiers how to "properly" deal with transgenders? How much time was wasted creating those training modules for commanders and soldiers? How much time was spent trying to figure out how to enact these misguided policies? What could our service members have done with that time?

The military is not a social experiment. It is not a normal job. It is significantly more physically, mentally, and emotionally demanding than regular jobs and careers. Military leaders need to wake up to the effects their leadership is having on the force, how they are weakening the ranks and creating distrust among those who serve.

Now that transgenders are allowed to openly serve, nonbinary or gender-fluid service members are looking to be next. Nonbinary service members—meaning those who do not identify as a specific sex—are not officially recognized in the military, although it can be assumed that most commanders are looking the other way even now. Nonbinary individuals usually prefer "they" or "them" as their pronouns, and their gender preference is different from their biological sex they were born with. They often consider themselves "gender X" when filling out questionnaires on forms. Some nonbinary people, similarly to transgender individuals, use hormones to alter their body and voice. But the Pentagon's stance on nonbinary service members is basically just no-recognition. This lack of policy regarding nonbinary individuals will likely change soon, probably before the 2024 election. The Pentagon has already funded a nonbinary study to help leaders make a decision on acknowledging a policy.[35] But what's different about this compared to the policy on transgenders—where, once individuals transition, identify as the opposite sex, and make it official in DEERS (Defense Enrollment Eligibility Reporting System) system, they then show their gender preference on their ID cards? At that point, they are allowed to use the sex-segregated restrooms and shower facilities of the opposite sex, but the sex with which they "identify." DEERS is a military database that contains service members' personal information (as well as their families') and is what is used for health care. Anything that applies to their sex, as labeled on their ID card and as identified in DEERS, is now available for that transgender person. Without restrictions.

It's different with nonbinary individuals, because instead of male or female, they have created a new bureaucratic gender-category twist. So you would have males, females, and gender X. That in turn comes with an entire new set of issues that the DOD would need to navigate, including medical care, whether or not these individuals will sleep in male or female barracks, and where they will stay when the unit goes to the field. What new accommodations for bathrooms, showers, and sleeping quarters will be necessary? What about on deployments? Does that person have to shave if he's picked that day to identify as a woman? What about hairstyles? What dress uniform will the person wear?

Serving is a privilege, not a right. And serving comes with a rigid set of requirements and standards not to be bent or adjusted or to fit a category, whether existing or fanciful. If you are disqualified, it's likely because whatever condition has prevented you from serving will take away from mission focus. It's not a personal reflection on you, it's just not conducive to the military and its mission.

Nowadays, military leadership refuses to accept this. Leadership continues to blame outward factors for its failures and hardships. If it doesn't look inward and admit that many of its problems are self-inflicted, then this identity and leadership crisis will only grow. And it is burgeoning even now. Military leaders are doubling down on a woke ideology that is focused on a ridiculously complex gender neutrality. This madness continues to damage the fighting force.

CHAPTER 8

Another Forgotten War

*"And when the war is done and youth stone dead,
I'd toddle safely home and die in bed."*

Siegfried Sassoon

After 9/11, the military had a focused involvement in Afghanistan. There was a clear mission: Hunt for Osama bin Laden and al-Qaeda, who had planned the deadliest attack on American soil since Pearl Harbor. Bin Laden had initiated it from Afghanistan and remained in hiding there, so the mission was to locate and destroy him, as well as al-Qaeda and any entities who harbored his terrorist organization. The hunt went on for over a decade, and in the meantime the United States got to nation-building in Afghanistan, with the intent of completely toppling the Taliban. The goal became blurred, and mission creep settled in. Twenty years later, failure to live in reality, terrible leadership, and unrealistic expectations resulted in the most seismic and catastrophic foreign policy failure in our lifetime.

Osama bin Laden had been killed on May 2, 2011, in a compound in Abbottabad, Pakistan, by a special operations team later revealed as Navy SEALS and 160th Night Stalkers. President Obama approved the operation. The news broke soon after, and the world cheered that the terrorist leader of al-Qaeda, responsible for the 9/11 attacks, was now dead after a ten-year manhunt by US forces, while al-Qaeda and the Taliban in Afghanistan were now dispersed. The US military had accomplished what it had set out to do a decade prior: it killed the leader of al-Qaeda, decimated the terrorist organization, and successfully prevented it from using Afghanistan as a home base to plan or to launch more terrorist attacks against the United States.

This was supposed to be a pivotal moment in the Afghanistan War, a war in which thousands of US service members had lost their lives and tens of thousands more had been injured. But nothing happened. The war did not change. The strategy did not change. Instead, the fight continued as if nothing pivotal had happened. The military was trapped in its own cycle of failure in a war whose mission was now as unclear as ever.

NATO took over the ISAF (International Security Assistance Force) on August 11, 2003.[1] The initial strategy was entirely lacking.[2] First, the mission was to destroy al-Qaeda and hunt down Osama bin Laden, then to destroy the Taliban, then any local leaders who undermined the US government. The strategy changed again, this time with the aim to prop up the Afghanistan government, creating and building an Afghan military with the hope that in doing so, the Afghan Security Forces (ASF) would become self-sufficient. The theory was that ASF could prevent terrorist organizations from using their nation as a safe haven to plot future terror attacks. In 2009, the top commander in Afghanistan, General McCrystal, said, "If the people are against us, we cannot be successful. If the people view us as occupiers and the enemy, we can't be successful and our casualties will go up dramatically."[3]

Afghanistan had become a never-ending campaign for "hearts and minds."

Between 2009–2011 there was a significant surge in military and civilian resources as well as funding. But in 2011, after the surge, it became clear that no progress had been made despite the substantial resource increase. The United States wasn't winning hearts and minds. The United States wasn't winning at all. By the time bin Laden was killed, NATO and the United States had been fighting for nearly eight years. It was a mess, and no one knew what to do.

So the leadership doubled down. More time. More money. More troops. We'd heard it all before. At the end of 2014, ISAF's mission was officially over, and they handed it off to the Afghan forces, who assumed the lead on all security operations. This changed the definitions of the US combat role, but the actual fight raged on just the same. On January 1, 2015, NATO began a non-combat operation called Resolute Support. By NATO's definition, the war was essentially over. The Afghans were in charge, and there were no more combat missions. Now the mission was to provide ASF with training, advice, and assistance.

Except American soldiers were still dying in combat. While the military told Congress and the American people that US troops were accompanying the ASF to oversee missions, the US military was actually conducting these missions themselves. In some cases, the US military would bring ASF on its missions so that they could be called "advise and assist missions" and still be within legal parameters. In reality, the Afghanistan government and military were a shell propped up by the Americans. There are many accounts of special operations soldiers holding ASF partners by the shoulders, pointing them in the right direction, and telling them to shoot. Or having them knock on the door of a compound, then US soldiers would push past the ASF partner and complete the mission.

The Taliban was created in the early 1990s and was comprised of Afghan mujahideen, a CIA-backed Islamic fighting group that fought the Soviets in the late 1970s to the late 1980s in the Afghan War. While the Taliban had a smaller-sized fighting force and was less equipped than the US military or the ASF, its members were driven by an ideology that required them to never give up, as they had not after twenty years of war with the Soviets.

On the other hand, the Afghan military had hundreds of thousands of soldiers, was well-equipped, funded by the United States, and led and trained by NATO and the US military. But there were endemic issues with corruption and attrition, and this crippled its long-term capabilities. The attrition rate was astounding. Most of the Afghan force was illiterate and had little to no education. Some didn't know how many members were in their own family. Some would randomly leave patrols while out on missions to take naps under trees. This is who US soldiers were tasked with training to become an elite fighting force. Low morale, senior-level and commander corruption, and listing ghost soldiers on the payroll so commanders could pocket their salaries were also among the many problems plaguing the Afghan military. Meanwhile, the Afghan military lacked the ideological component that is necessary to be devoted to a cause. Many within the ranks were suspicious of their political leaders and didn't trust their commanders. Even so, many fought valiantly for their country, thousands died, and many did their best out of the hope for a better Afghanistan. Many worked side-by-side with the US military for years as interpreters or commandos, or assisted the government in other ways. Leaders often viewed the war through the lens of US military capabilities, not through the lens of a failed state with an illiterate population. Even though this type of system would never work on a group of tribal, uneducated, and in some cases primitive people, that didn't stop leaders from continuing to push the narrative of optimism, while at the same time reducing transparency into what was really going on in the countryside.

In 2015, the embarrassed Pentagon even classified the data surrounding the Afghan military, including the size, strength, and casualties of the Afghan security forces—raising multiple red flags about the unprecedented lack of transparency surrounding the program that leaders continued to rave about as essential to the success of the future of Afghanistan.[4] Flaws continued to grow in the training program. Afghans clearly were nowhere near ready to assume responsibility for securing their own nation.

The ultimate failure was that of the military leaders who had sold the idea to politicians that we could succeed in Afghanistan and portrayed Afghanistan's government and military capabilities as much different from what they actually were. The boldness of the lies of these politician generals was astounding. Generals and Pentagon officials touted the idea of women's rights, freedom, girls going to school, and peace. They proclaimed that the weak Afghan government and military were on the way to being self-sustainable in one of the most brutal and unforgiving regions in the world.

Even when they knew the truth, the generals misled Congress anyway.

Year after year, commander after commander. The litany of feel-good rhetoric is amazing—and appalling.

In 2011, General David Petraeus, commander of NATO/ISAF-US Forces Afghanistan, testified before Congress that in developing the Afghan security forces, "we have seen significant progress in this area . . . they fought with skill and courage."[5]

In 2011, Army lieutenant general William Caldwell, the commander of US and NATO training command in Afghanistan, told the Council On Foreign Relations, "We've made tremendous strides, incredible progress. . . . They're probably the best-trained, the best-equipped and the best-led of any forces we've developed yet inside of Afghanistan. They only continue to get better with time."[6] He went on to predict that because of the amazing strides the Afghan military had made, US combat troops would be able to leave Afghanistan by the end of 2014.

In 2012, Marine Corps general Joseph Dunford told Congress, "When I look at the Afghan national security forces and where they were in 2008, when I first observed them, and where they are today in 2012, it's a dramatic improvement,"[7] and is therefore optimistic about the status of the war.

In 2013, Army general Mark A. Milley, deputy commander of US forces in Afghanistan, also had a favorable viewpoint of the war. He said, "I am much more optimistic about the outcome here, as long as the Afghan security forces continue to do what they've been doing. . . . If they continue to do that next year and the year after and so on, then I think things will turn out okay in Afghanistan."[8]

In 2015, General John Campbell, commander of Resolute Support/ISAF-US Forces Afghanistan, said, "[T]he Afghan National Defense & Security Forces (ANDSF) have proven themselves to be increasingly capable. . . . Our Afghan partners have proven they can and will take the tactical fight from here."[9]

But the writing was on the wall. The Afghan government would never be able to stand independently without being led by the US military and funded by the US taxpayer. That is what the situation on the ground in Afghanistan has always been. The end result in Afghanistan would be the same whether we left in 2011 or 2021. The Taliban would likely destroy the Afghan military, topple the government, and again rule Afghanistan.

None of this was a secret. None of this was a surprise. Starting in 2009, the United States funded the Special Inspector General for Afghanistan Reconstruction (SIGAR) to report on the status of the Afghanistan War and the progress of reconstruction efforts. SIGAR provided quarterly reports, special reports, and audits. The true, hard facts are all there. Yet the weight of generals testifying on Capitol Hill that Afghanistan could be something other than a graveyard of empires carried more credence than the fact-filled SIGAR reports. There was no accountability, and Congress kept funding the war.

The Afghanistan War was a war of lies that could never be won. In reality, there was no chance of Afghanistan being what the US military and other officials said it could be. Once Osama bin Laden was killed, it was time to go.

During President Trump's administration, he pledged to start the process to end the nearly two-decade-long war in Afghanistan. In 2020, he delivered the Doha agreement, a peace deal between the United States and the Taliban to end the war in Afghanistan.[10] When he left office, the troop level was down to twenty-five hundred.[11]

Then on April 14, 2021, President Joe Biden announced that he would be the one to end the war in Afghanistan. The Department of Defense would begin the process of withdrawing the final twenty-five hundred troops in May, and the war would be concluded by September 11, 2021, the twentieth anniversary of the war.

On July 21, 2021, twenty-six days before the fall of Afghanistan, General Mark Milley was still spouting off talking points from a decade before. At a Pentagon press briefing, he stated, "The Afghan security forces have the capacity to sufficiently fight and defend their country."[12] This statement came after the Taliban had made significant advances all over the country.

A little over a month before the fall of Afghanistan, at a White House press conference on July 8, 2021, President Biden responded to a reporter who asked if there were parallels between the Afghanistan withdrawal and what happened in Vietnam. "The Taliban is not the south—the North Vietnamese army. They're not—they're not remotely comparable in terms of capability. There's going to be no circumstance where you see people being lifted off the roof of [an] embassy in the—of the United States from Afghanistan. It is not at all comparable."[13]

In fact, the images would be much worse.

In the same briefing, when asked about how it was that the Taliban was at its strongest point militarily in the last twenty years, President Biden responded, "Relative to the training and capacity of the ANSF and the training of the federal police, they're not even close in terms of their capacity."[14] The truth was that the Taliban was militarily at its most robust and capable point. Twenty years of effort later, trillions of dollars spent,[15] thousands of American lives lost, and over twenty thousand wounded, and the Taliban was stronger than ever. As we would soon find out.

Apart from the long-term strategic failures, the decision to withdraw all remaining troops from Bagram airbase in early July was an operational failure that proved to be the final blow. Aside from the 650 troops guarding the embassy in Kabul, thousands of troops left overnight with little notice to their Afghan counterparts.[16, 17] They went in the dead of night and cut off the electricity, and the new Afghan base commander wasn't even aware all US forces had departed until hours after they left.

The decision to close Bagram initiated a chain reaction that led to the chaotic evacuation. It was a crucial airbase. In the twenty years since the military's arrival in 2001, it had been strategically upgraded. It was a former Soviet airbase, had multiple runways, and tactically was much easier to defend than Kabul. The base had established logistics and security measures, and the surrounding geography provided a good defense. It also wasn't in the middle of an urban sprawl.[18]

General McKenzie, the CENTCOM commander and the general who was overall in charge of the operations in the Middle East, including Afghanistan, said the "Bagram option went away" because President Biden had ordered all military troops to leave Afghanistan, and therefore the military wouldn't be able to use Bagram as an airport for mass personnel evacuations without increasing the troop levels that would be required to secure the base. McKenzie went on to testify to the House Armed Services Committee that he "did not see any tactical utility" in keeping Bagram. General Milley, chairman of the Joint Chiefs of Staff, seemingly contradicted him, probably in order to back up the president's statement, saying that using the Kabul airport, not Bagram, to evacuate civilians had *always* been the plan.[19, 20]

Once Bagram was closed, the US military was left with only one evacuation option: relying on Kabul (HKIA), a far less favorable alternative, and this left limited options for contingencies. HKIA is in an urban setting and is surrounded by most of the city of Kabul. Many of its entrance points are bottlenecked, and its only runway is unfortified and was primarily used for commercial air travel.[21]

When Bagram Air Base fell, it was estimated that between 5,000–7,000 prisoners were released by the Taliban from its prison. Many of these prisoners had ties to ISIS, al-Qaeda, or the Taliban, had significant fighting experience, and posed a major threat to the United States.[22]

Over 7.1 billion dollars' worth of US military equipment was left behind at Bagram. That included ammo, ground vehicles, aircraft, night vision goggles, and over 316,000 weapons, to the tune of $512 million.[23] Most operational equipment fell into the hands of the Taliban after the withdrawal, many of which were later likely sold on the black market. Even worse, the United States left behind sensitive biometric data of thousands of Afghans with connections to the US government or military. The data contains fingerprints, iris scans, addresses, photos, relatives, and more identifying and tracking information.[24] This has likely been used by the Taliban to hunt down, torture, and kill those who aided the United States during the twenty-year war.

Roughly six hundred and fifty Marines remained to guard the fourteen hundred Americans at the US embassy in Kabul. That put over two thousand Americans in severe danger of a potential hostage situation if the US embassy remained open after the Taliban surrounded Kabul.[25] This set the stage for Saigon 2.0, the same situation President Biden said not even a month prior could ever happen. President Biden rapidly ordered more US troops to assist with the withdrawal, totaling around six thousand troops at HKIA.[26] A few days before the collapse, military assessments were still confident that Kabul would face increasing pressure from the Taliban fighting forces as early as September and that the entire country could collapse in a few months.[27, 28]

Contingency planning is a significant part of mission planning, but it seems as though after the military left Bagram in July, everyone just threw their collective hands in the air and took the attitude that "it's probably not going to be that bad." A complacent intelligence community, the White House, DOD, State Department, and all other entities involved didn't seem to consider what would happen once they got Americans to the airport. Nor did they plan for any other contingencies, no matter how obvious.[29, 30] The fact that the Taliban might seize control of the access points to the airport as well as the entire perimeter if they took Kabul did not seem to have occurred to anyone. When this happened, the Taliban controlled who came to and went from the airport. While President Biden was asked if he trusted the Taliban and said no, he operated the withdrawal as though he did. By all evidence, it certainly seems that the Biden administration trusted the Taliban to do as they said they would. The additional troops ordered to Kabul immediately before the collapse were not part of contingency planning, however, but were a response to the situation spinning out of control. The United States had waited too long to react. By the time the additional troops arrived, it was too late.

What happened next was a failure of epic proportions. By August 15, 2021, the Taliban had taken Kabul. The entire Afghan government crumbled—organized and empowered by two decades of war, over $2 trillion, 2,448 US service members killed, and over twenty thousand wounded—collapsed in a matter of weeks.[31] The White House ordered evacuations to the Kabul airport for all US personnel still remaining throughout Afghanistan. The scene was indeed eerily familiar to April 29, 1975, in Saigon at the end of the Vietnam War. US military helicopters were landing on the rooftop of the US embassy in Kabul to evacuate its diplomats, much like US military helicopters did in Saigon almost fifty years earlier.[32] This time, due to ubiquitous cell phones and social media, people around the world were watching this all in real time.

And it got worse, as image after image revealed. Videos went viral of frantic Afghans clinging to US military aircraft as they sped down the runway for takeoff. Images of bodies falling from the sky flooded the internet, and photos of frightened, desperate crowds on the runways creating conditions that prevented aircraft from safely taking off or landing. It was clear things were out of control.

The city panicked as word got around that the Taliban was now in power. Afghans were lining up at ATMs to withdraw as much money as possible. Fleeing Afghans had to weigh the option of trying to pass through Taliban-controlled checkpoints to get to the airport gates and chance an evacuation against trying to make it to the border to escape. But by this point, the Taliban controlled all of the border crossing points, and the possibility of traveling by road looked grim. Afghans trying to get out on refugee status or SIVs (Special Immigrant Visas), many of whom were interpreters or who had worked with the US military or government, were trapped in Kabul, and there was an active door-to-door manhunt by the Taliban to capture them. People desperately rushed to the airport, hoping to be the lucky ones who would make it out. Parents were giving up their babies and passing them to the crowd towards the airport perimeter fence on the chance their child would get out alive. Many Afghans were being beaten in the streets by the Taliban. The Afghan people were desperate.

By August 26, 2021, Afghans had crowded outside the airport gates for ten days hoping to get a chance to make it on a flight out of the country. Their desperation was beyond belief. At 1750 local time in Kabul, a massive explosion ripped through Abby Gate, one of the entrances into HKIA. Thirteen US service members were killed when the ball bearings of the ISIS-K suicide vest tore through them: eleven Marines, one sailor, and one soldier. One hundred seventy Afghans were also killed. Biden's incompetent and failed withdrawal was now deadly. Thirteen Americans would not come home to their families. It would later be confirmed by national security officials to Congressman Ken Calvert of California that the ISIS-K suicide bomber who killed thirteen American service members and 170 Afghans during the withdrawal of HKIA had been one of the prisoners who was released from the Bagram prison just days prior by the Taliban.[33]

After the ISIS-K suicide attack, the US military started collaborating with the Taliban to get their help securing the HKIA perimeter and to prevent ISIS from gaining access to the airport or American service members. The US military was now working with the Taliban, the terrorist organization they had been fighting for twenty years, including just days before.

General Frank McKenzie, CENTCOM commander, said the Taliban and the United States now had a "common purpose."[34] General McKenzie said he wanted to use the Taliban as a tool as much as possible. The Taliban was now conducting screening of Afghans in the outer cordon of HKIA—many of those "screened" had worked with the United States throughout the war and were a significant target to the Taliban. That's right: Afghans who were targets of the Taliban for having worked with Americans, and were trying to escape the Taliban, now had to get cleared by the Taliban to gain access to HKIA.

On August 29, three days after the ISIS-K suicide bombing, the US military conducted a "defensive" airstrike by drone on a target that the military said posed a significant and imminent threat to HKIA airport. CENTCOM said, "US military forces conducted a self-defense unmanned over-the-horizon airstrike today on a vehicle in Kabul, eliminating an imminent ISIS-K threat to Hamid Karzai International Airport."[35]

But that's not what happened. The US drone strike killed ten members of the same family—three adults and seven children, the youngest two years old. The father who was killed was an aid worker.

For three weeks, the Pentagon maintained that they killed a member or facilitator of ISIS-K. The chairman of the Joint Chiefs of Staff, General Milley, called the attack a "righteous strike."[36] It wasn't until one week after a *New York Times* investigation exposed it as a mistaken civilian target that the military admitted its mistake. A secondary explosion had occurred at the time of the strike. Officials tried to use that as proof that the car was carrying explosives. The investigation revealed it was likely a large propane tank nearby.[37]

Once the Pentagon was outed for wrongly killing civilians, General Mckenzie said, "We now assess that it is unlikely that the vehicle and those who died were associated with ISIS-K or were a direct threat to US forces. . . . I offer my profound condolences to the family and friends of those who were killed."[38] He also added that he was "fully responsible for this strike and this tragic outcome."[39]

Military and political leadership had not looked this incompetent since the Vietnam War. The disaster was unspeakable. It was time to end the war, but the way the leadership went about it produced an extreme failure filled with outright ineptitude and tragic consequences. The operation gave our enemies an inside view of our priorities, vulnerabilities, and horrible decision-making at the top. It showed our potential future partners how we treat those who help America. By every measure, we abandoned our allies in Afghanistan and allowed their families to be hunted down, tortured, and killed.

A year and a half later, on March 8, 2023, the House Foreign Affairs Committee held its first hearing on the investigation into the botched Afghanistan withdrawal. It was a painful and heart-wrenching testimony. One of the forty-five wounded in the Kabul attack was Marine Sgt. Tyler Vargas-Andrews, who was leading his sniper team in assisting the evacuation. He recalled the events of August 26, 2021, when the ISIS-K suicide bomber killed thirteen service members and 170 Afghans, and wounded forty-five more outside of the Kabul airport at Abby Gate:

"I opened my eyes to Marines dead or unconscious lying around me. . . . My body was overwhelmed from the trauma of the blast. My abdomen had been ripped open; every inch of my exposed body except for my face took ball bearings and shrapnel," Vargas-Andrews said.[40] He lost two limbs and multiple organs and has had forty-four surgeries because of the blast. He was twenty-five years old at the time.

"Our military members and veterans deserve our best because that is what we give to America. The withdrawal was a catastrophe, in my opinion, and there was an inexcusable lack of accountability and negligence," Vargas-Andrews said. "The eleven Marines, one sailor, and one soldier that were murdered that day have not been answered for."[41]

He went on to discuss how prior to the blast, his team was not given authorization to shoot the bomber once they ID'd him in the crowd. His team had received precise information about what the bomber looked like. Vargas-Andrews went on to ask intel, since they had such specific information, why did they not apprehend him sooner? The response he got from intel was chilling: "I was told the asset could not be compromised." Meaning that the CIA or DIA or whatever group they were getting their intel from chose to protect their asset over potentially saving lives. After his conversation with intel, Vargas-Andrews's sniper team made a positive ID on the suicide bomber. He reported to his higher command, assuring them they had an easy shot to take out the target. "Pointedly, we asked him for engagement authority and permission. We asked him if we could shoot. Our battalion commander said, and I quote, 'I don't know.'"[42]

Vargas-Andrews went on to testify that "plain and simple, we were ignored. . . . Our expertise was disregarded. No one was held accountable for our safety."[43]

This is such a perfect example of a collective failed decentralized command that resulted in the murder of thirteen American heroes. Military commanders won't take risks anymore. They've been conditioned to shirk off decisions rather than making the call themselves. The military preaches mission command, the concept of decentralized command through mutual trust and disciplined initiative.[44] Mission command is even counted as a tenant of Army leadership policy. Despite this, the military routinely fails to implement it, and never more so than in the scenario that Sgt. Vargas-Andrews describes at the Abby Gate. Instead, there is the domino of events where leaders abdicate decisions, leaving them to their bosses.

That battalion commander received information that his snipers had a positive ID on the target and an "ease of fire" shot to take him out.[45] The sniper was taking disciplined initiative. He wasn't requesting to shoot randomly into a crowd—he was asking to take out a suicide bomber that posed a known and grave risk to American service members at Abby Gate and to Afghans trying to evacuate.

Why was a positive ID of the target not approved when requested by the sniper? Why didn't commanders have that authority, or worse, the confidence to make that decision? Apparently mission command wasn't articulated to commanders to operate with intent that was likely to protect Abby Gate and the perimeter of Kabul International Airport. It appears that lower-level commanders on the ground did not have authority delegated by his commanders—who needed their superiors' support in order to have the confidence to make those fast and crucial decisions. It was chaos, that's for sure. But if field commanders don't have the authority to approve taking out a suicide bomber, then that shows a more deadly leadership breakdown.

We've trained a generation of leaders to phone a friend through satellite communications so they don't have to make hard choices. The military now has arrived at a culture where no one wants to make a tough decision, and that indecision can be deadly. Technology has made it too easy for soldiers to call the boss, ask him to make a decision, and seemingly absolve a subordinate of any responsibility. It's a culture of passing the blame. Military leaders have become reliant on the instant technological ability to seek approval. It is easier and safer than making a call themselves.

Major General Donahue, who at the time was the division commander of the 82nd Airborne and the ground commander of the HKIA evacuation,[46] got promoted after the botched withdrawal. A little over six months after the withdrawal, Donahue received his third star and became Lieutenant General Donahue. He took command of the 18th Airborne Corps headquartered at Fort Bragg, North Carolina. He also received significant overnight media attention. A photo taken under night vision goggles that showed General Donahue walking onto the last airplane to leave Kabul was released by the Pentagon as the "the last American soldier out of Afghanistan."[47] He was praised. Articles were written about him.

There are plenty of failures to go around, from the mismanagement of the war, to misleading and even deceiving the public and Congress about the status of the war, to the lead-up of the withdrawal. This includes the State Department and multiple other government agencies. This creates undeniable resentment and distrust for the military among the American people. It furthers the civilian-military divide.

The Afghanistan Papers were published by the *Washington Post* on August 31, 2019. They were an exposé of how the Pentagon didn't have a strategy to win in Afghanistan, and the Pentagon's expectation to lose the war. It was a bombshell. The Pentagon was selling a war with no end state, strategy, or logic. But it got surprisingly little coverage outside of the D.C. political news crowd, who merely found it embarrassing. When the public became outraged, Congress would have to become outraged, and worse, would have to explain why it was continuing to vote for a defense budget that funded a war that the Pentagon admitted privately was failing and was probably unwinnable. Congress is supposed to be accountable to the people. But when the public outrage never came, Congress didn't have to care either.

The Afghanistan Papers revealed the open secrets of the Afghanistan War and the leadership failures that many suspected for so long. The Papers released documents that proved that the war was unwinnable—and leaders admitting it. They also revealed that when decisions were made, they were not made in the context of Afghanistan, the current status of the Afghan military, and security forces and their capabilities. Instead, many decisions were made in the fantasy realm where Afghanistan was an already functioning and successful democracy. In reality, it was anything but that. The Papers also revealed that the American people had been regularly misled. John Sopko, the head of the Office of the Special Inspector General for Afghanistan Reconstruction (SIGAR), even acknowledged "the American people have constantly been lied to."[48]

Lieutenant General Douglas Lute, the former Afghanistan–White House war czar during the Obama and Bush administrations, said, "If the American people knew the magnitude of this dysfunction . . . 2,400 lives lost. Who will say this was in vain?" He continued, "What are we trying to do here? We didn't have the foggiest notion of what we were undertaking."[49]

In an August 2016 interview revealed by the Afghanistan Papers, Bob Crowley, a retired Army colonel and senior counterinsurgency advisor from 2013–14, said, "Truth was rarely welcome" in leadership circles in Afghanistan and that headquarters "just wanted to hear good news, so bad news was often stifled." He went on to say, "Every data point was altered to present the best picture possible."[50]

The revelations brought by the publishing of the Afghanistan Papers should have been one of the biggest stories in decades, yet was largely dismissed by most. It got a twenty-four-hour news cycle, and then it was gone. It wasn't until after the spectacularly botched withdrawal that Congress started to take issue with the war they had been funding for twenty years.

At the same hearing on Afghanistan during which Marine Sgt. Tyler Vargas-Andrews spoke, Army combat medic Aiden Gunderson, who was also at Abby Gate, testified, "I want Americans to know the truth: that the Afghanistan withdrawal was an organizational failure at multiple levels."[51]

House Foreign Affairs Committee chairman Mike McCaul concurred in his opening statements of the hearing: "What happened in Afghanistan was a systemic breakdown of the federal government at every level—and a stunning, stunning failure of leadership by the Biden administration," McCaul said, adding that more than a thousand American citizens and an estimated two hundred thousand Afghan allies and partners were left behind.[52]

"This was an abdication of the most basic duties of the United States government to protect Americans and leave no one behind," McCaul continued. "I want every gold and blue star family member and every veteran out there watching this today to know that I will not rest and this committee will not rest until we determine how this happened, and hold those responsible for it accountable."[53]

Of course, none of this has happened, and may never.

Retired Lieutenant Colonel Scott Mann, a Special Forces veteran and founder of Task Force Pineapple—an organization composed of veterans who volunteered to help assist with the evacuation—testified, "We might be done with Afghanistan, but it is not done with us. The enemy has a vote. If we don't set politics aside and pursue account-ability and lessons learned to address this grievous moral injury on our military community and right the wrongs that have been inflicted on our most at risk Afghan allies, this colossal foreign policy failure will follow us home." He also noted that the Afghanistan withdrawal and Abby Gate bombing caused a mental health crisis among Afghanistan War veterans, calling it a "mental health tsunami." He continued, "73 percent of our Afghan war veterans say they feel betrayed by how this war ended" and that there was an 81 percent spike in VA hotline calls following the withdrawal.[54]

In 2022, CENTCOM's (Central Command, the command respon-sible for the AOR area of operation of Iraq and Afghanistan) Abby Gate 15–6 investigation excused it own actions, saying that the loss of life "was not preventable at the tactical level without degrading the mission to maximize the number of evacuees" and "was not the result of any act of omission or commission by forces on the ground."[55]

The Pentagon had once again cleared itself of any wrongdoing, regardless of how evident and overt its failures were.

It's been almost three years since the world witnessed the most cataclysmic foreign policy disasters in generations. What's almost as horrific as the war and evacuation is that no one has been held culpable for these leadership failures. Just as bad, multiple generals, including the chairman of the Joint Chiefs, either grossly overestimated the strength of the ASF, underestimated the weakness of the ASF, or flat-out lied. There have been zero consequences. Those in charge were completely wrong about the situation—and they still continued to be promoted and placed in charge of larger US foreign policy and military operations.

The massive disconnect between the Pentagon elite in Washington, D.C. and military commanders on the ground in war zones is a serious problem and continues on. Senior officials create unrealistic expectations and insurmountable challenges for those service members tasked with fighting their wars. Strategies that sounded good in Washington, D.C. and at the Pentagon translated into disaster, death, and defeat.

To this day, no one has been held accountable for Afghanistan.

CHAPTER 9

Rewriting History

"Those who control the present control the past, and those who control the past control the future."

George Orwell

What is so great about the military? Everyone is the same color: everyone is green. You wear the same uniform and the same American flag patch on your right shoulder. You bleed the same color, you feel the same struggles and pain in training, you support and motivate each other to get the job done. Why? Because those who make it through training are on the same team with the same mission. You rely on each other to succeed, to live, to save each other when things go wrong. The military takes away divisive backgrounds and differences and brings everyone together as a team. That's how teams work. The model of basic training or boot camp is to break everyone down to the same level and then build everyone back up, together. The American military is the world's biggest melting pot of people of different backgrounds, education, upbringing, and classes, all working for the same purpose. Yet today's military leaders want to take away what makes the military great and unites the force, and instead focus on issues that divide and weaken in a misguided attempt to ingratiate themselves with politicians.

In September 2020, in its final few months, the Trump administration announced that the Department of Defense, among other federal institutions, was banned from implementing Critical Race Theory (CRT) and white-privilege teachings that were "divisive, anti-American propaganda."[1] In a tweet, President Trump said, "A few weeks ago, I BANNED efforts to indoctrinate government employees with divisive and harmful sex and race-based ideologies. Today, I've expanded that ban to people and companies that do business . . . with our Country, the United States Military, Government Contractors, and Grantees. Americans should be taught to take PRIDE in our Great Country, and if you don't, there's nothing in it for you!"[2]

Racial-sensitivity training expanded during the Obama administration and quietly carried over into the Trump administration until Trump squashed it in 2020. In 2011 President Obama issued an executive order that created an initiative called the Government-Wide Inclusive Diversity Strategic Plan. Five years later in 2016, the Obama administration rolled out the second phase of the executive order, the New Inclusion Quotient, which requires agencies to provide training on cultural education, unconscious bias awareness, and inclusion.[3]

A few weeks prior to President Trump's tweet, a letter sent to all federal agencies from Office of Management and Budget director Russell Vought explained the reasons for banning this type of training in the federal government. It had already costs millions of dollars to push a divisive, anti-American ideology. Vought explained, "[E]mployees across the Executive Branch have been required to attend training where they were told that 'virtually all White people contribute to racism' or where they are required to say that they 'benefit from racism.' According to press reports, in some cases these training efforts have further claimed that there is racism embedded in the belief that

America is the land of opportunity or the belief that the most qualified person should receive a job." The letter went on to cancel and remove all federal contracts supporting that type of training and forbid using taxpayer dollars on any training or suggestion that "the United States is an inherently racist or evil country."[4] To make the order official, later the same month President Trump issued an executive order "to combat offensive and anti-American race and sex stereotyping and scape-goating [that] similarly undermines efficiency in Federal contracting. Such requirements promote divisiveness in the workplace and distract from the pursuit of excellence and collaborative achievements in public administration."[5] It was logical and made common sense to remove CRT and other divisive training.

On his very first day as the President of the United States, on January 20, 2021, President Joe Biden revoked President Trump's order[6] and issued a new executive order, 13985, titled "Advancing Racial Equity and Support for Underserved Communities through the Federal Government."[7] This being one of his first executive orders, obviously Biden thought that racial equity was one of the most important issues to tackle. Never mind the other pressing matters that were threatening our national security, the opioid crisis, or a US infrastructure that was falling apart. But Biden's order went a step further than President Obama's did.

The order read, "The federal government's goal in advancing equity is to provide everyone with the opportunity to reach their full potential. Consistent with these aims, each agency must assess whether, and to what extent, its programs and policies perpetuate systemic barriers to opportunities and benefits for people of color and other underserved groups."[8] Biden's new order actually required agencies and the federal workforce to promote diversity, equity, and inclusion within the ranks. The order required agencies to audit themselves to determine whether or not there were barriers in place that prevented minorities from equity, opportunities, and benefits and then remove those barriers of discrimination.

Equity is different from equality. In the context of diversity and inclusion, the two have very different meanings. Equality is a bedrock of our nation and ensures that people are treated equally with the same opportunities. Almost everyone agrees the Americans should receive equal opportunity to try or pursue, without the guarantee of success. Just trying doesn't ensure a certain outcome. Equity, on the other hand, means equal outcome—or else. It's a guarantee that if one does not rise up, then another will be pulled down.

Since Biden took office there has been a drastic push to change the culture in the military. The military has spent nearly six million man-hours on training like CRT and diversity and inclusion, including a full "stand-down day" to learn about alleged white supremacy and extremism within the ranks.[9] Our military forces are full of patriotic Americans willing to lay down their lives in defense of their fellow service members and our country. It is disgusting to have military leadership require training that tells our service members that *they* are the perpetual problem plaguing the country, and that our nation is systemically racist.

Because of President Biden's executive order, Critical Race Theory is now integrated throughout the federal government and the military and is bleeding over into our education system. The theory has been around for decades, dating back to the 1970s after the civil rights legislation in the 1960s. What's new is the push to teach revisionist history, as fact, into all aspects of the federal government, including the military. CRT is viewing history through racism and believing that systemic racism is still running rampant through every aspect of society. CRT teaches that the US system and its institutions were designed to favor white people and oppress minorities. CRT has a goal: it is to dismantle the system of oppression and rebuild a more just society. This incredibly divisive ideology labels white people as evil oppressors and minorities as victims of white people's oppression.[10] Those in favor of CRT usually believe that race is not biological, but rather a social construct that was invented or inherited, like wealth.[11] They believe that race, like gender, is something that people choose.

Combatting this alleged state of affairs requires using the past and a fictional version of history to push a radical ideology into institutions that creates discord and sows racial tensions. When CRT is taught within the education system and universities, it is usually mandated training. So it is at the Air Force Academy: instead of students being taught critical thinking to better their decision-making, cadets are told what to think. This instruction comes with a flood of offenses white people are said to inflict daily, such as exercising white privilege, committing microaggressions, and possessing unconscious bias.[12]

In 2021, the chief of Naval Operations, the Navy's highest officer, Michael Gilday, released his Professional Reading Program, which contained a list of multiple left-wing, anti-American books including *The New Jim Crow*, *Sexual Minorities and Politics*, and *How to Be an Antiracist*. All three books promote divisive, anti-American agendas. Multiple members of Congress sent letters of concern to the CNO about the official reading list. The reading list exists to help educate and train sailors. Representative Jim Banks of Indiana, who is also a Naval Reserve Officer, demanded the CNO remove the books from the official reading list. He refused, stating that sailors need "self-reflection."[13] In 2020, Ibram X. Kendi, the author of *How to Be an Antiracist*, tweeted, "I keep saying there's no such thing as being 'not racist.' We are either being racist or antiracist. And in order to be antiracist, we must, first and foremost, be willing to admit the times we are being racist."[14] Kendi goes on to say that when someone says he is not a racist, he is actually in a state of pathological denial. This is clearly stated in Kendi's book, the very book that the CNO recommended all sailors read.

In an exchange with Senator Tom Cotton of Arkansas, Gilday said that "We need critical thinkers in the Navy and throughout the military." I couldn't agree more. The Navy does need critical thinkers who are able to think outside the box and not succumb to groupthink. The CNO continued, "In our enlisted force, again, we not only think outwardly but inwardly so that they make hopefully objective, facts-based decisions and draw conclusions in a world that is increasingly more difficult to get an unbiased view at a really tough problem."[15] How much does the CNO really like critical thinkers? We've seen what happens to service members who speak out against the CRT ideology. They are charged, fired, demonized. So when the CNO says he trusts sailors to be able to read something critical and draw their own conclusion, he actually means they are likely racists and need to do some self-reflection.

How does reading a book that says capitalism is racist actually unite and better prepare the Navy for war in the Pacific with China? It doesn't. It divides. It distracts. And it's pushing woke ideology on the Navy.

But as bad as the CNO's 2021 reading list was, the military service branch that is really leading the way when it comes to CRT indoctrination is the Air Force. Air Force leadership has certainly prioritized its woke agenda over flight training, which was evident when the Air Force F-16 missed its first shot at an unidentified object flying over Lake Huron on February 12, 2023. The Sidewinder air-to-air missile cost $400,000 a piece.[16] Shots are missed. It happens. But when the Air Force has been prioritizing CRT and woke appeasement over the past few years, it opens the door for criticism that maybe the force as a whole should be focusing more on their jobs instead of focusing on their inner feelings.

In 2020, the Air Force Air Education and Training Command launched its first video, "Microaggressions," in a series called "Seeking to Understand." The series focuses on phrases that may be offensive to people and attempts to address racial disparity. The video features airmen who are able to tell their stories about hurtful things that have happened to them in the past. Making and watching this is a distraction and a waste of taxpayer dollars that could be better spent on military preparedness.[17]

The Air Force is emboldened by its diversity agenda. In July 2021, an Air Force Academy professor, Lynne Chandler García, wrote an op-ed published in the *Washington Post* titled, "I'm a Professor at a US Military Academy. Here's Why I Teach Critical Race Theory." In the op-ed she wrote, "Critical race theory provides an academic framework to understand these nuances and contradictions. It helps students identify the structural racism and inequality that has been endemic in American society. And it provides methods for deconstructing oppressive beliefs, policies and practices to find solutions that will lead to justice."[18] These are our future military leaders, who are being taught that America is an inherently racist country. How are they expected to fight and potentially die for this country if they are taught that it isn't that great, and is perpetually racist anyway? There will be long-term effects on the next generation of the fighting force. It is destructive. It coddles cadets and teaches them to be mentally soft and to despise the country they have signed up to serve. It is glaringly obvious from the past few years that individuals are *not* allowed to have differing points of view when it comes to CRT. You either fall in line and comply or you're labeled a racist and bigot. The term "critical thinking" is being used as cover to indoctrinate the force with a destructive ideology, and so far it's working.

In 2021, the Air Force Academy confirmed that it was requiring incoming cadets to participate in diversity and inclusion training, which included watching a diversity and inclusion video that was supportive of Black Lives Matter. Black Lives Matter is a radical activist organization whose founders are devout Marxists.[19] In 2022, as part of a slide presentation in diversity and inclusion, cadets were instructed not to use the terms "mom" and "dad" because the words are not inclusive enough. Also that using the phrases "color-blind," or "I don't see color," or "we're all just people" was no longer acceptable. And if you made a mistake, you should be humble about it. If you need further instructions—which, apparently, if you think everyone is equal, you definitely do—you can visit the official Air Force "D&I reading room."[20]

In July 2020, the secretary of the Air Force announced that the Air Force and Space Force had created a new task force to tackle the "issue of racial, ethnic and other demographic disparities and their impact on the forces."[21] Brigadier General Troy Dunn, who at the time was the director of the Diversity and Inclusion Task Force, said, "Racial disparity is a national issue that impacts all facets of American life and we will not rest until our Airmen and Space Professionals feel like they truly belong and are thriving in an organization that values diversity and equality."[22]

According to its website "currently, racial and ethnic minorities make up 40% of the US population but only 24% of the Air Force officer corps."[23] The Air Force wants to increase the minority representation within the officer ranks. Instead of opening these positions up to everyone and selecting based on merit, the Air Force wants to focus on skin color. Imagine you are in a commercial airliner and an Air Force plane is flying in the same traffic pattern as your airliner. Imagine that in order to properly sequence a landing, the Air Force pilot needs to understand the complex instructions from the air traffic controller. Perhaps the weather is bad and the air traffic controller makes a mistake and tells both your commercial airliner and the Air Force plane to land at the same time. Would you rather have the very best pilot with the best judgement and reflexes, or would it be better if the pilot were selected based on arbitrary characteristics, such as skin color? If that best person is someone with a skin color that fits into a certain demographic, great, but skin color should have nothing to do with selection.

Air Force recruiting also decided it was time to tackle "unconscious bias." From a video on the Air Force recruiting channel on YouTube: "As airmen in the US Air Force, it's our duty to acknowledge our biases whether we realize they exist or not. . . . Let's listen. Let's talk. And let's change for the better."[24] It is downright terrifying in an age of peer-adversarial competition that our essential defenders in the Air Force should be shamed with the ridiculous notion of unconscious bias.

In the fall of 2022, the Air Force Academy sent out an email to cadets regarding information about the Brooke Owens Fellowship, a nine-week paid program, encouraging cadets to apply. The application reads in part, "If you are a cisgender man, this program isn't for you."[25] In plain language, this means that heterosexual men are not eligible. The application stated, "If you are a cisgender woman, a transgender woman, nonbinary, agender, bigender, two-spirit, demigender, genderfluid, genderqueer, or another form of gender minority, this program is for you."[26] It is quite worrisome that the Air Force Academy, an elite military institution, is promoting DEI programs such as this. The material itself makes it clear that DEI is meant to take priority over mission-essential tasks.

The Air Force Academy is coddling the next generation of Air Force leaders. In combat, the enemy isn't going to check with you to see how you are feeling before he shoots at you. He is not going to care what pronouns you use or what gender you are identifying as. He is going to try to kill you, along with all of your buddies fighting next to you. One of the Air Force's primary responsibilities is to prepare its airmen to face that enemy. In the heat of combat, you won't care what pronoun the person next to you calls you as long as he tries to take out the enemy and save your ass.

In 2021, the Office of Naval Intelligence (ONI) created an "Artwork Working Group" to address the lack of inclusivity and diversity representation in artwork at the National Maritime Intelligence Center. The ONI chief of staff sent out communications that encouraged employees to send in suggestions for artwork that would make people feel valued. They ended up adding art reflecting Native American Indians, Hispanics, and Africans.[27] The office that is responsible for all naval intelligence and tracking the Chinese naval fleet and its capabilities surely has better things to do.

In 2022, General Milley and Defense Secretary Austin testified in front of the House Armed Services Committee hearing on the defense budget. It quickly went off the rails when Congressman Matt Gaetz of Florida asked some straightforward questions.

Gaetz started by inquiring of Secretary Austin what the Department of Defense thought about CRT. Not one to miss an opportunity for a fiery exchange with a member of Congress that might produce a juicy headline, General Milley interrupted the defense secretary—only to be shut down by Gaetz. Secretary Austin then responded, "I don't know what the issue of critical race theory is." After being enlightened, the secretary went on to say, "We do not teach critical race theory. We don't embrace critical race theory, and I think that's a spurious conversation."[28] Only the year prior, an Air Force Academy professional confessed to teaching CRT in a *Washington Post* op-ed.[29] It shows a disconnect from leadership at the Pentagon—either willful or honest—from the troops if the secretary of defense doesn't know something so pervasive is happening within his force.

Congressman Michael Waltz exposed his contradictions by citing a letter he previously received from the superintendent at West Point that stated that the military academy did teach a course on Critical Race Theory. He went on to discuss a mandatory seminar at the United States

Military Academy, in which the instructor taught about white rage and understanding whiteness.[30]

Later in the hearing, General Milley stated that he does think Critical Race Theory is important. He went on to say, "I want to understand white rage, and I'm white, and I want to understand it. . . . So what is it that caused thousands of people to assault this building and try to overturn the Constitution of the United States of America? What caused that? I want to find that out." Sounding like a CRT spokesperson, Milley implied that January 6 had something to do with "white rage."[31] And in doing so, he confirmed that Secretary Austin's extremism stand-down day was, in fact, political in nature.[32]

It didn't end there. Milley continued, "I've read Mao Zedong. I've read Karl Marx. I've read Lenin. That doesn't make me a communist. So what is wrong with understanding—having some situational understanding about the country for which we are here to defend?" Milley said. "And I personally find it offensive that we are accusing the United States military, our general officers, our commissioned, noncommissioned officers of being, quote, 'woke' or something else, because we're studying some theories that are out there."[33]

So the top general in the United States gets personally offended by an elected representative and member of Congress who, when representing his constituents, asks a question about a radical ideology being forced on our troops. Why so defensive? Why so angry? Why is he attempting to shame the congressman by implying that military leaders shouldn't be questioned or criticized? The US taxpayer does pay his salary, after all.

General Milley went on to remind the committee that military academies are universities and should be treated as such. Yes, they are universities, but the highest ranking officer in the military should know that the service academies should not be treated as normal universities. The service academies are charged with developing elite military leaders and officers who, at a very young age, will be responsible for leading men and women into combat. Do you think troops want leaders on the battlefield who studied innovative strategies to win battles and bring their men home, or leaders who studied how America is a systemically racist nation whose institutions were created to hold minorities back while advancing white people?

General Milley knows the type of influence he carries on military culture when he speaks. Other senior leaders take note. Milley understands this—which makes his loose and careless communication about CRT that much more of a problem. It was transparent what Milley wanted to do, which was clear himself of any association with President Trump. He wanted to come out swinging for the other side and make it clear as day that he was not a "Trump guy." He spent the entire hearing attempting to make this clear.

Congressman Michael Waltz sent a letter to the superintendent of West Point in April 2021 addressing concerns about information and material he had received from West Point cadets, their families, and soldiers about mandatory diversity, equity, and inclusion training, as well as critical race theory, in its curriculum. In the letter, Congressman Waltz said, "I was provided a presentation slide from one of the workshops with the title of 'White Power at West Point' and 'Racist Dog Whistles at West Point.' Additionally, another presentation slide shared with me depicted a lecture by Dr. Carol Anderson of Emory University with the title 'Understanding Whiteness and White Rage.'[34]

"Additionally, I understand that on September 24, 2020 the entire corps of cadets was required to report to Michie Stadium for your address as superintendent and to hear from a cadet panel. In this session, an active duty female colonel described to the Corps how she became 'woke' to her white privilege, and felt guilty for the advantages of her race. At this same assembly, white police officers were described

as murderers with no context or court documents provided to corrobo-
rate the anecdotes of police brutality."[35]

In combat, everyone bleeds the same color on the battlefield.
Everyone. Teaching cadets to focus on the color of people's skin instead
of being blind to it is not preparing them for leading troops in not-so-
distant wars. It's time to bring back an old military saying: "Train as
you fight." The color of your skin isn't going to matter on the battlefield,
and it shouldn't matter at home either.

Members of the military, including cadets, are not activists. If
activism is an individual's goal in life, then he or she shouldn't be
attending a military academy. He or she can attend any other university and find plenty of that type of opportunity. It does not belong
in military institutions. Service academies exist to train our nation's
future leaders, who will lead men and women into combat to destroy
our nation's enemies. They can't do that if they are taught to hate their
country, each other, and themselves.

CHAPTER 10

The All-Volunteer Force Is Failing

"Only individual faith in freedom can keep us free."
Dwight D. Eisenhower

1.3 million active duty military members are currently serving our nation.[1] That's less than 1 percent of the population who serve in the military at any given time. US citizens view military service significantly differently than in the Vietnam era, when service members were demonized for serving their country. Some American citizens took political and foreign policy anger and frustration out on those that wore the uniform, even though many were forced into service through a mandatory draft. They were called baby killers and were even spit on. Thankfully, things are different today. People rightfully air their foreign policy grievances at politicians who send people to war, instead of at the people who are forced to fight in them. But that said, Americans are less connected to those who serve than ever before. America's youth are not interested in serving in the military, and this is reflected by the dismal recruiting numbers from nearly all military branches.

So what happens if Americans no longer want to serve? Who will fight our wars that American politicians are addicted to? Even if the

US government uses a draft to attempt to fill numbers during a time of war, the quality of those serving would be subpar and likely not effective enough to win a kinetic ground war against China. To add to the delusion, a 2020 post on the Department of Defense website says, "There's been a consensus among Defense Department leaders that the all-volunteer force is working and is attracting America's talented, physically fit and motivated youth."[2] That is completely out of touch from an institution that required the all-volunteer force to carry the load of two wars over almost twenty years. The all-volunteer force is failing. The DOD could not be more wrong or more out of touch with reality.

The Selective Service Act—what some people incorrectly refer to as the draft—was enacted into law in 1917, although there have been varying levels and types of conscription since the Revolutionary War. Prior to the Civil War, each state was responsible for its own militia, and the militia was not regulated or enforced at the federal level. Standards were quite loose, and all men aged eighteen to forty-five were eligible, although there was no method of enforcement. This did not change until 1863.[3]

The War Department (what is now the Department of Defense) was in charge of enacting the Enrollment Act of 1863, which required involuntary service in the military from all men—the draft. For registration, military groups were instructed to go house to house in search of men eligible to serve, as well as hunt down those thought to have deserted. This created significant contention among the civilian population, and in some cases even caused hostility.[4]

By World War I, the Provost Marshal General, who served under the War Department, was responsible for the operation and organization of the draft. Once the Draft Act of 1917 was enacted to expand the military by conscription, 24 million American men were registered. Originally the age set for the draft was twenty-one to thirty, but expanded to eighteen to forty-five. Over 2.6 million men were drafted, with another two million who volunteered.[5]

Society strongly preferred isolationism following World War I and mostly had minimal interest in any military involvement against Germany, Japan, or Italy.[6] Yet the nation was connected to the war through citizens who were linked to those who had served in World War I, including many who lost husbands, brothers, or sons. After 1940, it became increasingly clear that Great Britain and other allies would not be able to fend off the Germans on their own. During World War II, the selective service system was an independent federal entity, separate from the War Department, whose director reported directly to the president. On September 16, 1940, President Roosevelt signed a new military draft into law called the Selective Training and Service Act. For the first time in our nation's history, Americans were drafted during peacetime.[7] Men who were selected through a lottery had to serve in the military for one year. Of the 15 million Americans who fought in the US military in World War II, it is estimated that around 66 percent were draftees. By the end of World War II, 45 million men had registered for the draft, with 10 million of those men being drafted and inducted into the military. When the war was over, the draft law expired. But a few years later in 1948, with the threat of communism and the start of the Cold War, the draft was reinstated.[8]

The Korean War drafted a little over 1.5 million Americans during its span. Additionally, there was the Physicians and Dentist Draft Act, which required "7,054 physicians and 3,799 dentists" to be drafted. Conscientious objectors were required to serve for two years, in jobs that the local registration boards deemed necessary in areas that were vital to national interest, like health and safety.[9]

The Vietnam War–era draft left a significant and negative impression on the US population. A strong anti-war movement grew and was met with many protests across the nation. Twenty percent of men in uniform were drafted during the Vietnam War, totaling about 1.85 million men.[10]

After the Vietnam War, the draft ended in 1973,[11] but selective service registration remained until 1975, when its registration ceased.[12] But by 1979, it was clear that the United States needed an option for back-up in case of an emergency or if the all-volunteer military wasn't enough. In 1980, Selective Service registration for men aged eighteen to twenty-five began again.

Today, the military selective service is still active. It is a felony if one fails to register for the program by the time he is twenty-six years old. A conviction carries a penalty of a $10,000 fine and up to five years in prison.[13] Once you are twenty-six, you are no longer eligible for registration, and if you haven't registered, aside from legal trouble, you won't be eligible for government jobs or student loans, and could face losing citizenship or loss of federal and state government benefits. Within thirty days of a male's eighteenth birthday, he is required to register through the Selective Service, by mail through a postcard or online. There is an eight-year grace period. Therefore, every male US citizen and immigrant aged eighteen to twenty-five is required to register, with very few exceptions. Undocumented immigrants, handicapped individuals, and transgender women must also register. If a draft is enacted, individuals will be selected by lottery and birth year. Then individuals are assessed for mental and physical fitness before being required to join the military. In 2017 the selective service turned over two hundred thousand names and addresses to the Department of Justice for failing to register,[14] though no one has been indicted since 1984.[15]

In 2017, the National Defense Authorization Act required the creation of the Commission on Military, National, and Public Service to study the future of the selective service system, including whether women should be required to register. It also assessed ways to increase service interests in the name of national security. For years, there had been increasing calls to study whether selective service registrations should be required when an all-volunteer force had been sustained since the Vietnam War. After two and a half years of research, the commission recommended that mandatory selective service registration remain. The report concluded "that maintaining an active, mandatory registration system mitigates the level of potential risk to the Nation and protects the critical functions and procedures that safeguard a fair, equitable, and transparent draft process."[16]

It is apparent that much of the United States population has stepped away from any sort of citizen sense of duty when it comes to the defense of our nation. Americans are grateful other people serve. The fallout of Vietnam and now the fallout of Afghanistan had significant impacts. Also, the way veterans were treated both by the federal government and society during Vietnam and its aftermath had significant effects echoing for decades. The draft has become a dirty word. The military has since prided itself on having an all-volunteer force, and has even publicly advertised that this is the only way forward for the US military. Military leadership may be rethinking that now.

An all-volunteer force for a nation of our size is quite rare and not something that is guaranteed. The post 9/11 wars have shown how fragile and unstable an all-volunteer military can actually be during a time of war, especially against a peer adversary rather than mere terrorist organizations. We're just now starting to see the effects.

After 9/11 the country saw a resurgence of patriotism, and it was reflected in recruitment numbers. But it quickly waned once the post-9/11 wars kicked off and the mismanagement and ineptness of Americans generals were revealed. Today, patriotism has dwindled.

In 2023, the *Wall Street Journal* released a poll that revealed a drastic change in American values from twenty-five years ago. Thirty-eight percent of Americans viewed patriotism as very important in 2023. This was down from 70 percent in 1998. What is even more starkly evident is how drastically it was reduced. In 2019, patriotism was polled at 61 percent, down from 70 percent in 1998. It dropped

23 percent in four years, compared to a 9-percent drop in the previous twenty-one years. That indicates a rapid decline of a society, a society that doesn't believe in its nation's principles and values, and whose citizens will not voluntarily sign up to defend these with their lives.[17]

Then came social media and an interconnected world that put military decisions on display for the rest of the United States in a much more intimate manner. This includes decisions following the COVID-19 vaccine mandate, which led the Pentagon to kick thousands of people out of the military, the botched Afghanistan withdrawal, double standards, and horrible leadership. The nation watched the civil-military divide grow.

We have the best, most technologically advanced equipment. Tactically our military is the best in the world. But its leadership can't seem to get out of its own way.

Good and proper civil-military relations have always been critical to recruitment and sustainability. Support for the military has had periods of strong national support such as during World War II, but also periods of discord, like the Vietnam War. A divide that is expanding as rapidly as that has detrimental consequences.

The economy has historically been a contributing factor in the quality and quantity of those interested in serving. When the economy is bad and jobs are hard to come by, Americans consider the military at a higher rate than when the economy is booming and jobs with benefits are more accessible. Additionally, the workforce has changed. After the COVID pandemic, the traditional work structure shifted drastically. People have gotten used to a remote work environment, or at least a flexible or hybrid one. Many jobs have adapted to entice people to come back to the office. In some industries, perks and benefits became somewhat swanky in order to gain the best talent. Gourmet breakfasts, lunch spreads, Poke bars, yoga classes, and even DJs were commonplace in a lot of new-age corporate headquarters. Alternatively? The military offers second-rate health care, toxic leadership, and wars without end. No one realistically expects the military to offer competitive alternatives to the tech industry, but the military is losing out on areas in which it can effect change, including the training cycle op-tempo. During the height of the Afghanistan and Iraq Wars, Army units would deploy to a combat theater, then return home and start a very rigorous training cycle because they knew as soon as they got home, they had to train new unit members for another combat deployment that was likely a little over a year away. It was a vicious cycle. Deploy, come home, train, deploy, on and on. Soldiers commonly said they wished their next deployment was sooner, just so they could get a break from training so intensely when in the United States between deployments. Military units are no longer deploying at the op-tempo they once were. Yet they continue a rigorous training schedule that is as exhausting as deployments. But the military has a problem with change, just like any other bureaucracy. Once it is in a certain cycle, it's full speed ahead, without asking any questions or thinking about changing the pace that is having such a negative effect on those serving.

The military has lost sight of why people want to join in the first place. Sure, some do so out of patriotism and a sense of duty to protect our nation; others join to be a part of something great, an exclusive brother and sisterhood; others to get special skills or money for college. Most service members want to work really hard and make a difference. People are willing to make sacrifices that come with military service, including potentially giving their life, because they believe in being a part of something great. But many today are seeing the reality of modern day military life, and they are saying, "No thanks." Through that lens, many Americans see drama, double standards, and equity over standards and merit.

Additionally, the veteran population in the United States is rapidly shrinking. As of 2021, there were 19 million veterans in the United

States.[18] That's just over 7 percent of the population. In 1980, 18 percent of the population were military veterans. Between 2000 and 2018, the veteran demographic was reduced by one third, from 26.4 million to 18 million. It is rare for everyday Americans to come in contact with someone who served.

According to Army Recruiting Command data, 50 percent of young Americans don't know anything about the military.[19] Department of Defense internal research found that 65 percent of young Americans don't want to serve because they fear the possibility of death or injury. Sixty-three percent don't want to serve because of the possibility of PTSD or psychological or emotional issues.[20] A lot of the American public gets its perceptions from Hollywood, from movies that portray service members and veterans in a manner that is not always factual. Many young Americas think veterans have physical, emotional, and mental issues as a result of their service. People often think that a significant percentage of military veterans are amputees, when actually less than 1 percent are traumatic amputees.[21] People also correlate veterans with PTSD and then stereotype them as broken. They think that these veterans have a difficult time transitioning back to the civilian sector. Worse, there is a perception that their military service makes them victims.

Another area that has damaged the civil-military divide is foreign policy. War has become a business and a career field. The military-industrial complex has turned into a revolving door of former administration officials, generals, and admirals who promote their products for the next conflict. Americans used to sign up to serve out of patriotic duty. But now many question why they would sign up to be cannon fodder as a part of a business strategy for generals to climb the ladder of post-military careers.

Seventy-nine percent of recruits have a family member who served.[22] Historically, families play a significant role in influencing a recruit's decision to join the military. This is a major problem because America, veterans included, has drastically lost confidence in the military in recent years. Poll after poll shows Americans continuing to lose trust in a once highly respected and trusted institution.[23]

Military veterans used to be a trusted and reliable demographic for recruiters. For too long the military has heavily relied on veterans to be its primary marketing and advertising tool. That works when veterans want to share their positive experiences and still trust the institution that they served in. But this is not happening anymore. Veterans aren't the recruiters they once were. This is not because they aren't capable; it's because they aren't willing. It's because they know the truth of what military service is like today.

I spoke to dozens of service members and veterans over the course of writing this book, and asked them all the same question: "After your service and seeing the modern military with your own eyes, would you promote joining the military to your children or to other people's children?" Every single person, without hesitation, said, "No." I did not go out seeking naysayers and the disaffected. On the contrary, nearly everyone I spoke with was an example of martial competence, accomplishment, and personal accountability.

And they all answered, "No."

One person said no, but that he might make an exception for the Air National Guard. A few said that they would actively try to *prevent* their children from serving. That is absolutely terrifying for our nation and the all-volunteer force. Military leaders have lost the trust and support of their subordinates. For many, serving in the military had previously been a family business. If you served, your children were much more likely to serve because you helped promote military service as an option.

But veterans don't want their kids serving as pawns in politicized war games designed to affect election cycles and polling. This is how bad morale has gotten. The military mismanaged the wars in the Middle East. Military leaders lied to Congress and presidents by painting a rosy picture that didn't exist of a war whose reality was lodged in the memories of those who served. Soldiers on the ground were held accountable for operating under very restrictive rules of engagement (ROE) yet generals were not held accountable for losing wars. In fact, most were promoted. This is an issue that is being dismissed by the Pentagon, yet many veterans believe toxic leadership is running rampant throughout the military.

Generals used to be able to rapidly rise within the ranks. If they were a rising star, it was rewarded. The number of generals and flag officers also used to be much smaller. But there has been rapid "rank creep" over the decades following World War II. Today, there are more generals than ever before. There are roughly nine hundred generals and/ or flag officers serving. This bloat causes significant micromanagement and adds layers of wasteful bureaucracy. It also delays decision-making and dilutes a more direct chain of command.[24] It unnecessarily expands the separation between the general and the troops. Additionally, support personnel are needed just to provide the required staff for every general officer.

Veterans see this.

Today's generals rarely go outside the wire in combat. They don't fight. On the rare occasions they do leave the safety and security of the fortified base, they are treated with kid gloves and it is a circus. Units spend days, weeks, as much time as they have to prepare for a general's arrival. In doing so, lower-ranking officers create a completely different reality than the one they live and work in daily. On the rare occasion generals go on combat missions, they get even more elaborate fake productions. They are led into meetings with soldiers who have been preselected and coached on how to act and what to say to a general. General visits are dog and pony shows. The general gets what he wants to hear and leaves feeling satisfied about the morale and status of his troops. But it's not a real portrayal of the status of the operational level.

Veterans are not fooled.

Generals these days only get fired for scandals or politics. This has allowed mediocre officers to rise to the highest ranks. How can leaders preach good order and discipline when there is no account-ability at their own level? People don't want to follow weakness. Weak leadership is dangerous and gets people killed, just as we saw with the Afghanistan withdrawal, where a Marine had a clear shot to take out the suicide bomber and was told he couldn't shoot—and as a result thirteen Americans were murdered. The secretary of defense went on to testify in front of Congress that he had no regrets when it came to the withdrawal.

Current service members and veterans have not forgotten these words and what they signified.

A dangerous culture of double standards and no accountability spreads toxicity through the ranks. This recent recruitment failure isn't even felt yet. Over the next twenty years we will see the effects. Families will no longer be a reliable demographic of recruitment. The nation will start to suffer the consequences of not being able to meet necessary manpower numbers for our national security.

Regardless of the severe disconnect between the American popu-lation and those who serve, Americans as a whole overwhelmingly respect those who are serving in the military and its veterans. For that, the post-9/11 veteran community is eternally grateful. The way service members are treated is rightly different in today's society compared to what service members had to endure during and after Vietnam. Vietnam War veterans know firsthand just how serious the conse-quences of a failed all-volunteer force are and how an entire nation pays for it.

A society without a direct connection to the military is dangerous. Even if an eighteen-year-old volunteers to serve the nation and claims that he is willing to die for it, that doesn't mean our society should overlook the responsibilities of our national military leadership to ensure that soldier's service is not taken for granted or that he isn't treated as cannon fodder. An all-volunteer force is not an excuse for unaccountable wars. Just because soldiers volunteer to join the military does not mean that those service members are easily expendable.

This isn't a Left versus Right or a Republican problem versus a Democrat problem. The widening civilian-military divide affects us all equally. This is an American problem. We will all feel the consequences. And fairly shortly if the course isn't corrected rapidly.

While military leadership evades any questions about what happens if the civilian-military divide continues to worsen and the military's recruitment numbers continue to fail, the answer is crystal clear: your sons, and potentially your daughters, too, will be drafted to fight in future wars.

What's worse is that, were the nation required to rely upon a draft, who could the country draft? The nearly 75 percent of Americans that are already ineligible for service because of obesity and other mental and physical health problems? Are those the Americans who are going to save our nation during a time of war with an adversary so brutal that a draft had to be enacted in the first place? No? Then who?

That is the dire situation that our nation is in. If nothing changes, it will not end well.

CHAPTER 11

The Alarm

"The only way to win the next world war is to prevent it."
Dwight D. Eisenhower

The 2018 National Defense Strategy was a historic document that, after decades, directed the United States military away from its focus on fighting terrorists in the Middle East.[1] The new strategy called out near-peer adversaries, namely China and Russia. But China is no longer a near-peer adversary. China is a peer adversary, which means that any kinetic action leading to a "hot" war would be the most catastrophic, destructive event that humanity has ever seen.

Incredibly, the US military shifted its focus, without delay, from Afghanistan to Ukraine, as if the twenty-year war and botched withdrawal never happened. Out with the old, in with the new. No reflection, no after action review, as the Army likes to call it. But there is a significant difference between fighting multiple wars in the Middle East versus the threats we face today across the globe. While threats from terror groups still exist, twenty years of fighting them have caused the United States to react in a distracted and apathetic manner as we face the rise of China and its aggression. Suddenly, that threat is here.

In early 2023, General Mike Minihan, commander of the US Air Force's Air Mobility Command (AMC), sent a memo with a dire message to the force, expressing the urgency of training and preparedness in the wake of a hot war with China, and that the force should be ready in two years.

"I hope I am wrong," the general wrote, "My gut tells me we will fight in 2025. [Chinese President] Xi [Jinping] secured his third term and set his war council in October 2022," Minihan's memo said. "Taiwan's presidential elections are in 2024 and will offer Xi a reason. [The] United States' presidential elections are in 2024 and will offer Xi a distracted America. Xi's team, reason, and opportunity are all aligned for 2025."[2]

His guidance to other commanders across his command is clear and urgent—commanders must ensure their units are prepared for the looming possibility of war if China invades Taiwan—and contains specific instructions, including going to the small arms shooting range and to "aim for the head," meaning shoot to kill and to ensure each airman's personnel affairs are legally in order in the event he or she is killed in battle.

The general goes on to discuss risk and to "run deliberately, not recklessly." He continued, "If you are comfortable in your approach to training, then you are not taking enough risk."[3]

The memo was future-dated for February 1, but was leaked and made its way to social media, where it quickly went viral. It stirred up a media frenzy in defense circles, with people wondering if the general knew something others didn't. Many criticized his memo, viewing it as a war cry, and argued it was provocative and aggressive. The Pentagon quickly threw the general under the bus and said, "These comments are not representative of the department's view on China."[4] Secretary Austin also attempted to minimize the general's comments by saying he doubts a Chinese invasion of Taiwan is imminent.[5]

But Minihan is known for being bold, telling it like it is, and speaking with authority. When discussing something this serious, people would be wise to listen. Also, as the commander of AMC, whose mission is to "provide rapid, global mobility and sustainment for America's armed forces,"[6] it seems pretty reasonable and even necessary for a general to send a memo to his troops to get them ready for a likely future conflict and to give them time to prepare.

Despite the Pentagon's criticism, Minihan is certainly not the first senior military leader recently to raise the alarm on the potential of future conflict with China.

When speaking to the Atlantic Council in October 2022, Admiral Michael Gilday, the chief of Naval Operations, said, "What we've seen over the past 20 years is that they have delivered on every promise they've made earlier than they said they were going to deliver on it."[7]

In the spring of 2021, Admiral Phil Davidson, then commander of US Indo-Pacific Command, testified in front of the Senate Arms Services Committee in regards to China, "I think our concerns are manifest here during this decade, not only on the development—the numbers of you know, ships, aircraft, rockets, etc. that they've put in the field—but the way they're advancing those capabilities as well in combination with everything that you just cited: Hong Kong . . . and Tibet, and a line of actual control in the South China Sea and the East China Sea." He went on to say, "I worry that they're accelerating their ambitions to supplant the United States and our leadership role in the rules-based international order, which they've long said that they want to do that by 2050. I'm worried about them moving that target closer." Davidson concluded, "Taiwan is clearly one of their ambitions before then. And I think the threat is manifest during this decade, in fact in the next six years."[8]

This rapid expansion of overt military capability and the prediction of China moving on Taiwan in the next six years was later dubbed "the Davidson Window."[9] Since then, the timeline has only narrowed. China's aggression towards Taiwan has increased at an alarming rate. Our current military shortcomings and weak leadership are visible for the world to see. China will attempt to take advantage of these weaknesses.

Regardless of who ends up being right about the timeline or what year it actually happens, it is expected that China is likely going to attempt to seize Taiwan, which may mean war with China.

One of the primary missions of the armed forces is to be in such a state of readiness and preparedness that our military's capabilities serve as a deterrent. That deterrence prevents conflict. It has worked for decades. Our adversaries think twice about getting involved in a conflict, or creating a conflict elsewhere in the world, for fear of bringing the United States and its highly capable military into the fight. And when deterrence doesn't prevent a conflict, having the best and strongest military in the world should allow for a swift victory. Optics matter. Stated priorities matter. When our adversaries see a strong, brutal fighting force, they are cowed. But when they see a softened, weakened military due to woke and green policies, this emboldens their military and opens the door to adversary aggression.

The military should be focusing all of its efforts on deterring and combating China and the alliances China is continuing to create.

A series of April 2023 Pentagon leaks revealed that China has hypersonic missiles that can reach Guam, home to a strategic US military base that is frequented by US aircraft carriers.[10] These missiles are extremely fast, extremely powerful, and can likely circumvent US missile defense systems. This means that aircraft carriers are basically out of the fight in the Pacific if a war breaks out. That completely changes the game. The United States has spent hundreds of billions of taxpayer dollars on aircraft carriers over the years, and now they are virtually unusable against our number one adversary because of China's ability to sink them at a fraction of the cost. China is not only outplaying our perceived strategic dominance, but it is able to do so with superior technology that is cheaper to produce and therefore can scale at a much higher rate.

During an April 2023 House Armed Services Committee hearing, Congressman Matt Gaetz of Florida denounced the leaks, but then asked a vital question: "Who's going to be punished more, the knuck-lehead who leaked this information, or the generals and admirals and so-called experts who have sat before this committee and the Senate for decades saying that these capabilities that we were funding with gajil-lions of dollars were going to sufficiently deter China?"[11] The answer is clear: the leaders responsible will never be held accountable.

In March 2023, the US Air Force unsuccessfully tested a hypersonic missile, the most recent acknowledgment of the delayed technology.[12] By comparison, as revealed in the leaked documents, in February 2023, China successfully tested a hypersonic missile that traveled thirteen hundred miles in twelve minutes.[13]

Perhaps the military's focus on CRT, gender identity, forced diver-sity, equity, and inclusion, drag shows on Air Force bases, and double standards isn't actually helping the military at all, despite the Pentagon constantly reassuring the American public that this ludicrous agenda is vital to military success. Perhaps, instead, a woke agenda has dam-aged the military to its core, as a deranged obsession with woke policies has caused the military to lose sight of critical threats and its mission. Now we have allowed China to pass us in advanced missile technology that could give them the strategic advantage on the battlefield. Woke military priorities have put our nation in a precarious position, one that we will pay for one way or another.

The downward spiral of our military is a problem that will affect every American. Woke policies have all but destroyed morale, recruitment, and retention and have effectively weakened our force structure and ability to fight wars.

Furthermore, the woke mindset has infected the next generation of our future military leaders. I recently spoke to cadets at a military institution about my leadership and combat experiences from my time in the military. Much of what I discussed was focused on challenges and hard work, with no special treatment during hardships in the face of adversity. After my speech was over, I did a Q & A with cadets and got some incredible questions. Many were from young women who were excited and proud to become commissioned officers in the military and wished to know the best way to prep. Others were looking for leadership tips. But I also received questions surrounding the topics of DEI (diversity, equity, and inclusion). One that stuck out to me was a young man that came to the microphone and asked me if my challenges would have been different if there were more people in my unit who looked like me. The question wasn't "Would more females make the unit better or more prepared to accomplish the mission?" It focused on whether more exposure to DEI would have made my life easier. Would I have had a better or easier time? Would my challenges and hardships have been different if more women were around? My answer was simple.

It's not supposed to be easy.

Having more people around you that "look like you" shouldn't have anything to do with whether you can accomplish the mission and be a reliable part of the team. And I didn't want it to. Every hardship I faced during training helped prepare me for combat and my mission. I faced plenty of hard times and plenty of "unfairness." That's life. You either figure out how to thrive despite what the world throws at you or you won't make it, and, frankly, you *shouldn't* make it.

Easy doesn't make you tough. So your training is supposed to be hard. Because being able to handle the hard times is what makes or breaks you. And you want to figure that out before you get to combat.

Your team needs to know if they can count on you in those hard times, of which there will be plenty.

But this new generation of leaders isn't thinking in this way. Because of this, they have been set up to fail. Many military leaders and professors alike are teaching them, training them, and indoctrinating them with woke policies and a woke mindset and are forcing a woke ideology on these new leaders. They are being taught that they should take the easy road. That they are special and unique. That it shouldn't be hard. That there should be a nurturing aspect to one's time in the service.

All of this teaches weakness. It teaches people to dwell on their hardships and make excuses, and that if something is ever hard, it must have to do with the color of their skin or their gender. Not only does this culture divide people, it is a lie. Life is hard. All of it. For everyone. Sometimes it's painful. Sometimes it hurts. But as you push through those hard times, you get tougher, more resilient. Tough times can make you mentally and physically tough. That's exactly what is needed for members of our fighting force. They should learn the truth, that our differences don't matter. What matters is that we are all Americans.

The military cannot deny that its diversity recruiting strategy has backfired. Men and women who see a weakened military with horrible leadership will seek out opportunities elsewhere in the civilian sector. We need Soldiers, Sailors, Airmen, and Marines who are ready to do harm to adversaries that threaten our way of life and our nation. The military must be made up of intimidating and lethal people, not activists.

Author G. Michael Hopf once wrote, "Hard times create strong men, strong men create good times; good times create weak men, weak men create hard times." If we aren't careful, these weak, woke men will lead us into very hard times indeed. There is still time to right the ship, but it must be done now before these woke policies entirely ruin the patriotic nature of our nation's military. There are still good people who want to change things, but we need strong leaders who aren't afraid to stand up, tell the truth, make a change, and make it quickly.

It will be a challenge like no other. The military has already become a generational indoctrination institution. Social engineering didn't happen overnight. It's been over a decade in the making. Reversing the damaged culture of the biggest government agency is not something that will happen overnight either. It will take strong leadership, with the backing of a president who understands how deep the rot is and that serious measures must be taken to fix it. It will take a secretary of defense who isn't lackadaisical about the Pentagon's failures or intimidated by military brass. It will take Congress understanding what is at stake and using the power of the purse to mandate change.

Most of all, it will include firing the majority of generals in order to help reduce the top-heavy and no-accountability culture plaguing the officer corps. It will mean getting rid of layers of bureaucracy and red tape that suffocates innovation and efficiency. It will mean cutting the government civilian workforce at the Department of Defense in half. It will mean civil service reform. It will mean refurbishing the promotion system, to retain top talent, into a system that is incentive-based, that focuses on merit and accomplishments and rewards hard work. And we must accomplish this enormously complex and difficult task while deterring our biggest adversary, China, which is ready to seize opportunities that will make it the dominant world power.

America isn't feeling the pain yet. The American way of life is still unaffected on the daily. Amazon deliveries still arrive. Food is still stocked on grocery store shelves. Power grids are still functioning. Americans can still heat their homes in the winter. The banking system remains operational. Until these comforts no longer exist, we will likely proceed on this collision course. The bad news is that our adversaries know this. The good news is the American spirit, even a dormant one, should never be underestimated.

This is the alarm. These are the flashing red warning lights. The military is in a free fall. The path is unsustainable. The warning signs are all there. Our adversaries are ready to exploit our weaknesses. Despite the clear damage and warning, the Pentagon's response has been to downplay every single warning sign and place blame for its problems on external factors.

On December 23, 1776, Thomas Paine wrote a piece titled "The American Crisis" in which he said:

> THESE are the times that try men's souls. The summer soldier and the sunshine patriot will, in this crisis, shrink from the service of their country; but he that stands by it now, deserves the love and thanks of man and woman. Tyranny, like hell, is not easily conquered; yet we have this consolation with us, that the harder the conflict, the more glorious the triumph. What we obtain too cheap, we esteem too lightly: it is dearness only that gives every thing its value. Heaven knows how to put a proper price upon its goods; and it would be strange indeed if so celestial an article as FREEDOM should not be highly rated.[14]

We have experienced trying times throughout American history. That is nothing new. Our nation will continue to face difficulties throughout its existence. The United States of America is the greatest country on earth. We cannot afford to sleepwalk through the blaring alarms of a failing military institution and the consequences that come with it. Without a strong military we don't have a country. It cannot be more simply stated than that. Our freedom and way of life are exactly what are at stake.

The alarms are ringing. Can you hear them?

NOTES

Introduction

1. Gillian Brockell, "She Was the Only No Vote against the War on Afghanistan. They Called Her a Traitor," *Washington Post*, August 17, 2021, https://www.washingtonpost.com/history/2021/08/17/barbara-lee-afghanistan-vote.

Chapter 1: We Have a Problem

1. Gertrude Chavez-Dreyfuss, "US Dollar Slumps after Weak Data; Markets Betting Fed Near End of Hiking Cycle," Reuters, April 4, 2023, https://www.reuters.com/markets/currencies/dollar-slides-sluggish-us-data-aussie-steadies-ahead-rba-2023-04-04.
2. "Transcript: Senate Armed Services Committee Hearing on Posture of USCENTCOM and USAFRICOM," US Central Command, March 17, 2023, https://www.centcom.mil/MEDIA/Transcripts/Article/3332606/senate-armed-services-committee-hearing-on-posture-of-uscentcom-and-usafricom-i.
3. "Why young Americans don't want to serve in today's military," Townhall.com. July 23, 2022. https://townhall.com/columnists/ambersmith/2022/07/23/why-young-americans-dont-want-to-serve-in-todays-military-n2610688.
4. Ibid.
5. Lolita C. Baldor, "Army Misses Recruiting Goal by 15,000 Soldiers," Associated Press, October 2, 2022, https://www.armytimes.com/news/your-army/2022/10/02/army-misses-recruiting-goal-by-15000-soldiers.
6. "Secretary of the Army and Chief of Staff of the Army Memorandum on Recruiting," Army.mil, July 20, 2022, https://www.army.mil/article/258577/secretary_of_the_army_and_chief_of_staff_of_the_army_memorandum_on_recruiting.
7. "Bonuses and Incentives," GoArmy.com, accessed March 14, 2023, https://www.goarmy.com/benefits/while-you-serve/bonuses.html.
8. "The Oath Project," United States Air Force Academy, accessed April 21, 2023, https://www.usafa.edu/cadet-life/clubs/oath-project.

9. Micaela Burrow, "Air Force Academy Touts New Program to Combat Politicization in the Military," *Daily Caller*, April 12, 2023, https://dailycaller .com/2023/04/12/air-force-academy-touts-new-program-to-combat -politicization-in-the-military.

10. Ibid.

11. US Department of Defense, "Department of Defense Releases the President's Fiscal Year 2024 Defense Budget," news release, March 13, 2023, https:// www.defense.gov/News/Releases/Release/Article/3326875/department-of- defense-releases-the-presidents-fiscal-year-2024-defense-budget.

12. Eleanor Watson, "More Than 1,100 soldiers at Fort Bragg Living in Mold- Infested Barracks," CBS News, August 26, 2022, https://www.cbsnews.com /news/fort-bragg-mold-barracks-relocation.

13. Karen Jowers, "'Poop Falling from the Ceiling' Shows Military Housing Issues Persist," *Military Times*, April 20, 2023, https://www.militarytimes .com/news/your-military/2023/04/20/poop-falling-from-the-ceiling-shows -military-housing-issues-persist.

14. "2022 Survey Summary," Reagan Presidential Foundation and Institute, accessed January 23, 2023, https://www.reaganfoundation.org/media /359970/2022-survey-summary.pdf.

15. "Report of the National Independent Panel on Military Service and Readiness," The Heritage Foundation, March 30, 2023, https://www.heritage .org/defense/report/report-the-national-independent-panel-military-service -and-readiness.

16. *Department of Defense Climate Risk Analysis* (Washington, D.C.: US Department of Defense, 2021), https://media.defense.gov/2021/Oct/21 /2002877353/-1/-1/0/DOD-CLIMATE-RISK-ANALYSIS-FINAL.PDF.

17. Idrees Ali and Phil Stewart, "Pentagon to Include Climate Risk in War Gaming, Defense Secretary Says," Reuters, January 27, 2021, https://www .reuters.com/article/us-usa-biden-climate-military/pentagon-to-include -climate-risk-in-war-gaming-defense-secretary-says-idUSKBN29W2PI.

18. "Executive Order on Tackling the Climate Crisis at Home and Abroad," The White House, January 27, 2021, https://www.whitehouse.gov/briefing -room/presidential-actions/2021/01/27/executive-order-on-tackling-the -climate-crisis-at-home-and-abroad.

19. Ali and Stewart, "Pentagon to Include Climate Risk in War Gaming, Defense Secretary Says."

20. "Statement by Secretary of Defense Lloyd J. Austin III on Tackling the Climate Crisis," US Department of Defense, January 27, 2021, https://www

.defense.gov/News/Releases/Release/Article/2484504/statement-by-secretary
-of-defense-lloyd-j-austin-iii-on-tackling-the-climate-cr.

21. Adam Sabes, "Biden Says Climate Change Is Bigger Threat to Humanity
Than Nuclear War: 'We're Going to Have a Real Problem,'" Fox News,
January 31, 2023, https://www.foxnews.com/politics/biden-says-climate
-change-is-bigger-threat-humanity-nuclear-war.

22. Paul D. Shinkman, "Top Military Officer Clarifies Biden's Threat Assessment:
Climate Change—but Also China and Russia," *US News & World Report*,
June 10, 2021, https://www.usnews.com/news/national-news
/articles/2021-06-10/top-military-officer-clarifies-bidens-threat-assessment
-climate-change-but-also-china-and-russia.

23. Ibid.

Chapter 2: Make Generals Great Again

1. Thomas E. Ricks, "General Failure," *The Atlantic*, November 2012, 54–65,
https://www.theatlantic.com/magazine/archive/2012/11/general-failure
/309148.

2. Ibid.

3. Lara Seligman, Tyler Pager, Connor O'Brien, and Natasha Bertrand, "Lloyd
Austin Emerges as Front-Runner to Lead Pentagon," *Politico*, December 7,
2020, https://www.politico.com/news/2020/12/07/lloyd-austin
-biden-secretary-defense-frontrunner-contender-443479.

4. Robert Burns, Michael Balsamo, Jonathan Lemire, and Zeke Miller, "Biden
Picks Lloyd Austin as Secretary of Defense," AP News, December 7, 2020,
https://apnews.com/article/lloyd-austin-secretary-of-defense-pick-b4e044e
062004bdcc8a5eb087ff74582.

5. "Lloyd J. Austin III," US Department of Defense, updated January 8, 2021,
https://www.defense.gov/About/Biographies/Biography/Article/2522687/
lloyd-j-austin-iii.

6. Valerie Jarrett, "Lloyd Austin to Lead US Central Command," The White
House, March 22, 2013. https://obamawhitehouse.archives.gov/blog/2013
/03/22/lloyd-austin-lead-us-central-command.

7. Richard Sick, "ISIS Captures Hundreds of US Vehicles and Tanks in Ramadi
from Iraqi Troops," Military.com, May 20, 2015, https://www.military.com
/daily-news/2015/05/20/isis-captures-hundreds-of-us-vehicles-and-tanks-in
-ramadi-from-i.html.

8. Luis Martinez, "General Austin: Only '4 or 5' US-Trained Syrian Rebels
Fighting ISIS," ABC News, September 16, 2015, https://abcnews.go.com
/Politics/general-austin-us-trained-syrian-rebels-fighting-isis/story?id
=33802596.

9. Luis Axelrod and Emily Rand, "Investigation Reveals CENTCOM General Delayed Intel on ISIS Fight Meant for the President," CBS News, September 22, 2016, https://www.cbsnews.com/news/did-a-centcom-general-delay-intelligence-meant-for-the-president.

10. Ibid.

11. Ibid.

12. Ibid.

13. Martinez, "General Austin: Only '4 or 5' US-Trained Syrian Rebels Fighting ISIS."

14. Shane Harris and Nancy Youssef, "Exclusive: 50 Spies Say ISIS Intelligence Was Cooked," *The Daily Beast*, April 14, 2017, https://www.thedailybeast.com/exclusive-50-spies-say-isis-intelligence-was-cooked.

15. "Centcom Accused of Manipulating Intelligence on ISIS Fight in Syria, Iraq," CBS News, August 11, 2016, https://www.cbsnews.com/news/centcom-accused-of-manipulating-intelligence-isis-fight-syria-iraq.

16. Howard Altman, "Defense Department IG Report Finds No Intelligence Falsification at CENTCOM." *Tampa Bay Times*, February 2, 2017, https://www.tampabay.com/news/military/macdill/defense-department-ig-report-finds-no-intelligence-falsification-at-centcom/2311667.

17. Ibid.

18. Harris and Youssef, "Exclusive: 50 Spies Say ISIS Intelligence Was Cooked."

19. Axelrod and Rand, "Investigation Reveals CENTCOM General Delayed Intel on ISIS Fight Meant for the President."

20. Matt Seyler, "Single Suicide Bomber Killed US troops and Afghans in ISIS-K Attack at Kabul Airport, Pentagon Finds," ABC News, February 4, 2022, https://abcnews.go.com/Politics/single-suicide-bomber-killed-us-troops-afghans-isis/story?id=82676604.

21. Nick Monroe, "Flashback: Gen. Milley Called US Drone Strike That Killed Children, Civilians 'Righteous.'" The Post Millennial, September 17, 2021, https://thepostmillennial.com/flashback-gen-milley-called-us-drone-strike-that-killed-children-civilians-righteous.

22. David Vergun, "Secretary of Defense Mandates COVID-19 Vaccinations for Service Members," Defense.gov, August 25, 2021, https://www.defense.gov/News/News-Stories/Article/Article/2746111/secretary-of-defense-mandates-covid-19-vaccinations-for-service-members.

23. Lolita C. Baldor, "Pentagon Drops COVID-19 Vaccine Mandate for Troops," AP News, January 10, 2023, https://apnews.com/article/politics-health-immunizations-lloyd-austin-covid-64752e91abbc3d707ee46373a3ce757e.

24. Mike Glenn, "'Defense Secretary Austin: 'No Regrets' over Chaotic US Withdrawal from Afghanistan," March 29, 2023, *Washington Times*, https://www.washingtontimes.com/news/2023/mar/29/lloyd-austin-no-regrets-over-chaotic-us-withdrawal.

25. Ibid. In December 2021, months after the withdrawal, Austin said he felt differently. When asked by Fox News's Bret Baier if he regretted anything about the Afghan withdrawal, he replied, "Bret, I regret the fact that we lost 13 of our finest at Abbey Gate. I regret that we lost 10 civilians in an errant strike." See Jon Brown, "Lloyd Austin Reacts with Awkward Silence When Asked If He Has Regrets about Afghanistan Withdrawal," Fox News, December 4, 2021, https://www.foxnews.com/politics/lloyd-austin-reacts-with-awkward-silence-when-asked-if-he-has-regrets-about-afghanistan-withdrawal.

26. Chelsey Cox, "Gen. Milley Feared Trump Might Launch Nuclear Attack, Made Secret Calls to China, New Book Says," *USA Today*, September 14, 2021, https://www.usatoday.com/story/news/politics/2021/09/14/gen-mark-milley-worried-trump-could-launch-nuclear-attack/8334915002; Teaganne Finn, "Gen. Milley Says He Wasn't Trying to Undermine Trump in China Call." NBC News, September 28, 2021, https://www.nbcnews.com/politics/national-security/gen-milley-defends-call-china-says-he-wasn-t-trying-n1280239.

27. Cox, "Gen. Milley Feared Trump Might Launch Nuclear Attack, Made Secret Calls to China, New Book Says."

28. Elizabeth N. Saunders, "There Was No Legal Way to Stop Trump from Ordering a Nuclear Strike If He Wanted To, Expert Says," *Washington Post*, September 14, 2021, https://www.washingtonpost.com/politics/2021/01/08/there-is-no-legal-way-stop-trump-ordering-nuclear-strike-if-he-wants-expert-says.

29. Sandy Fitzgerald, "Woodward's 'Peril': Milley Secretly Took Steps to Undermine Trump after Jan. 6." Newsmax, September 14, 2021, https://www.newsmax.com/us/bob-woodward-peril-mark-milley-nuclear-weapons/2021/09/14/id/1036383.

30. Cox, "Gen. Milley Feared Trump Might Launch Nuclear Attack, Made Secret Calls to China, New Book Says."

31. Ibid.

32. Finn, "Gen. Milley Says He Wasn't Trying to Undermine Trump in China Call."

33. "Chairman of the Joint Chiefs of Staff," Joint Chiefs of Staff, accessed April 22, 2023. https://www.jcs.mil/About/The-Joint-Staff/Chairman.

34. Sean Neumann, "Top Military General Apologies for His Role in Donald Trump's Controversial Church Photo-op," People.com, June 11, 2020, https://people.com/politics/general-mark-milley-apologizes-for-role-in-trump -church-photo-op.

35. Jeffrey McCausland, "Gen. Milley, Critical Race Theory, and Why the GOP's 'Woke' Military Concerns Miss the Mark," NBC News, June 28, 2021, https://www.nbcnews.com/think/opinion/general-milley-critical-race -theory-why-gop-s-woke-military-ncna1272558.

36. Christina Wilkie, "Top General Milley Reassured China, Others in Secret Calls as Trump Pushed Election Lies, Spokesman Says," CNBC.com, September 15, 2021, https://www.cnbc.com/2021/09/15/milley-held-secret -calls-with-china-others-as-trump-pushed-election-lies.html.

37. Goldwater-Nichols Department of Defense Reorganization Act of 1986, Pub. L. No. 99-433, 100 Stat. 980 (1986).

38. US Department of Defense. "DoD Directive 5100.01: Functions of the Department of Defense and Its Major Components," issued: December 21, 2010. https://www.esd.whs.mil/portals/54/documents/dd/issuances /dodd/510001p.pdf.

39. Monroe, "Flashback: Gen. Milley Called US Drone Strike That Killed Children, Civilians 'Righteous.'"

40. Paul Yingling, "A Failure in Generalship," Armed Forces Journal, May 1, 2007, http://armedforcesjournal.com/a-failure-in-generalship.

41. Bill Murphy Jr., "Midlevel Officers Weigh Risk, Reward of Criticizing Army Leadership," *Stars and Stripes*, February 8, 2012. https://www.stripes.com/ news/midlevel-officers-weigh-risk-reward-of-criticizing-army-leadership -1.168020.

42. Oriana Pawlyk, "Space Force CO Fired over Comments about Marxism, Military Now Subject of IG Probe." Military.com, May 20, 2021, https: //www.military.com/daily-news/2021/05/20/space-force-co-fired-over -comments-about-marxism-military-now-subject-of-ig-probe.html.

43. Ibid.

44. Ibid.

45. Department of Defense, "Political Activities by Members of the Armed Forces." DOD Directive 1344.10. Issued on February 19, 2008. https://www .esd.whs.mil/Portals/54/Documents/DD/issuances/dodd/134410p.pdf.

46. Roger Wicker, "Wicker Asks Department of Defense to Explain Firing of Space Force Commander," Senator Roger Wicker's website, May 21, 2021. https://www.wicker.senate.gov/2021/5/wicker-asks-department-of-defense-to-explain-firing-of-space-force-commander.

47. Calvin Shomaker, "Marine to Forfeit $5,000, Receive Reprimand for Criticizing Chaotic Afghanistan Withdrawal," *USA Today*, October 15, 2021, https://www.usatoday.com/story/news/politics/2021/10/15/marine-sentenced-criticizing-chaotic-afghanistan-withdrawal-scheller-lejeune/8471242002.

48. Katherine Fung, "Stuart Scheller to Forfeit Only One Month of $5,000 Pay after Judge Weighs Marine's Record," *Newsweek*, October 15, 2021, https://www.newsweek.com/stuart-scheller-forfeit-only-one-month-5000-pay-after-judge-weighs-marines-record-1639436.

49. *Stand-Down to Address Extremism in the Ranks* (Washington, D.C.: Department of Defense, 2021), https://media.defense.gov/2021/Feb/05/2002577485/-1/-1/0/STAND-DOWN-TO-ADDRESS-EXTREMISM-IN-THE-RANKS.PDF.

50. C. Todd Lopez, "Extremism Stand-Downs Focus on Oath, Not Data Collection," US Department of Defense, March 30, 2021, https://www.defense.gov/News/News-Stories/Article/Article/2555883/extremism-stand-downs-focus-on-oath-not-data-collection.

51. *Woke Warfighters: How Political Ideology is Weakening America's Military* (Washington, D.C.: Office of Senator Marco Rubio, 2021), 5, https://www.rubio.senate.gov/public/_cache/files/ee1d7a86-6d0c-4f08-bd15-24e5b28e54b7/3756824FA9C21B819BB97AAB16221530.woke-warfighters-report-3.pdf.

52. *2021 Demographics: Profile of the Military Community* (Washington, D.C.: Department of Defense, 2021), 23, https://download.militaryonesource.mil/12038/MOS/Reports/2021-demographics-report.pdf; *Woke Warfighters*, 5.

53. *Woke Warfighters*, 5.

Chapter 3: The Cost of Freedom

1. Tara Copp, "Recruiting a Generation with No Memory of Sept. 11," *Military Times*, September 11, 2017, https://www.militarytimes.com/news/2017/09/11/recruiting-a-generation-with-no-memory-of-september-11th.

2. Tom Philpott, "Military Update: Iraq War, Booming Economy Hampering Recruitment," *Stars and Stripes*, August 11, 2005, https://www.stripes.com

/news/military-update-iraq-war-booming-economy-hampering-recruitment
-1.36795.

3. Ibid.

4. *The Employment Situation: June 2005* (Washington, D.C.: Bureau of Labor
    Statistics, 2005), 1, https://www.bls.gov/news.release/archives/empsit
    _07082005.pdf.

5. Philpott, "Military Update: Iraq War, Booming Economy Hampering
    Recruitment."

6. Lisa Burgess, "$20,000 Bonus Offered to 'Quick Shippers,'" *Stars and
    Stripes*, August 2, 2007, https://www.stripes.com/news/20-000-bonus
    -offered-to-quick-shippers-1.67176.

7. Lizette Alvarez, "Army Giving More Waivers in Recruiting," *New York
    Times*, February 14, 2007, https://www.nytimes.com/2007/02/14/us
    /14military.html.

8. Corey Dickstein, "Troops Driven to Serve by 9/11 Now Lead a Generation
    That Doesn't Recall the Attacks," *Stars and Stripes*, September 9, 2021,
    https://www.stripes.com/branches/army/2021-09-09/military-recruiting
    -wars-on-terror-army-iraq-afghanistan-2825639.html.

9. https://www.stripes.com/theaters/middle_east/us-goes-one-year-without
    -a-combat-death-in-afghanistan-as-taliban-warn-against-reneging-on-peace
    -deal-1.661464.

10. Craig Whitlock, "A War with The Truth," *Washington Post*, December 9,
    2019, https://www.washingtonpost.com/graphics/2019/investigations
    /afghanistan-papers/afghanistan-war-confidential-documents.

11. Courtney Kube and Molly Boigon, "Every Branch of the Military Is
    Struggling to Make Its 2022 Recruiting Goals, Officials Say," NBC News,
    June 27, 2022, https://www.nbcnews.com/news/military/every-branch-us
    -military-struggling-meet-2022-recruiting-goals-officia-rcna35078.

12. Ronn Blitzer, "Army Suggests Soldiers Fighting Inflation Go on Food
    Stamps," Fox News, September 13, 2022, https://www.foxnews.com/us
    /army-suggests-food-stamps-soldiers-battling-inflation.

13. Patrick Donahoe (@PatDonahoeArmy), "This is me, yesterday, conducting
    a re-enlistment for one of the tens of thousands of women who serve in our
    Army. Just a reminder that @TuckerCarlson couldnt be more wrong.,"
    Twitter, March 10, 2021, 8:04 p.m., https://twitter.com/PatDonahoeArmy
    /status/1369831575916077056.

14. GEN Paul E Funk II (@PaulFunk2), "I agree Pat. Thousands of women serve
    honorably every day around the globe. They are beacons of freedom and they

prove Carlson wrong through determination and dedication. We are fortunate they serve with us," Twitter, March 10, 2021. 8:34 p.m., https://twitter.com/PaulFunk2/status/1369839062887108613.

15. Sergeant Major of the Army (@USArmySMA), "Women lead our most lethal units with character. They will dominate ANY future battlefield we're called to fight on @TuckerCarlson's words are divisive, don't reflect our values. We have THE MOST professional, educated, agile, and strongest NCO Corps in the world," Twitter, March 10, 2021, 10:00 p.m., https://twitter.com/USArmySMA/status/1369860649292083206.

16. Haley Britzky, "'We Aren't Going Away'—What Tucker Carlson Doesn't Get about Women in the Military," Task & Purpose, March 11, 2021, https://taskandpurpose.com/news/tucker-carlson-women-military-fox-news.

17. Ted Cruz, "Sen. Cruz: Pentagon Attacks on Tucker Carlson Damage US Military for Sake of Leftwing Ideology and Political Expediency," press release, March 14, 2021. https://www.cruz.senate.gov/newsroom/press-releases/sen-cruz-pentagon-attacks-on-tucker-carlson-damage-us-military-for-sake-of-leftwing-ideology-and-political-expediency.

18. Patrick Donahoe (@PatDonahoeArmy), "Hey @Hillsdale come get your boy.," Twitter, July 23, 2021, 7:45 p.m., https://twitter.com/PatDonahoeArmy/status/1418718910363361289.

19. Matthew Cox, "Army Redesigns Leave Forms to Simplify Time-Off Requests," Military.com. September 7, 2020, https://www.military.com/daily-news/2020/09/07/army-redesigns-leave-forms-simplify-time-off-requests.html.

Chapter 4: Silencing Dissent

1. Terri Moon Cronk, "Austin Outlines His Top Three Priorities on Defense: People, Teamwork," US Department of Defense, March 10, 2021, https://www.defense.gov/News/News-Stories/Article/Article/2526532/austin-outlines-his-top-three-priorities-on-defense-people-teamwork.

2. Lloyd Austin, "Secretary of Defense Message to the Force," Department of Defense, August 9, 2021. https://media.defense.gov/2021/Aug/09/2002826254/-1/-1/0/Message-to-the-Force-Memo-Vaccine-FINAL.PDF.

3. Lloyd Austin, "Memorandum for Senior Pentagon Leadership, Commanders of the Combatant Commands, Defense Agency, and DOD Field Activity Directors," Department of Defense, August 24, 2021, https://media.defense.gov/2021/Aug/25/2002838826/-1/-1/0/MEMORANDUM

-FOR-MANDATORY-CORONAVIRUS-DISEASE-2019-VACCINATION -OF-DEPARTMENT-OF-DEFENSE-SERVICE-MEMBERS.PDF.

4. Adrienne Bankert and Devan Markham, "Soldiers Fired over Vaccine Refusal Must Pay Back Bonuses," NewsNation Now, January 25, 2023, https://www.newsnationnow.com/health/coronavirus/vaccine/military -vaccine-bonuses.

5. "House Armed Services Subcommittee on Military Personnel Holds Hearing on COVID-19 DOD and Servicemember Impacts," Navy.mil, March 11, 2021, https://www.navy.mil/DesktopModules/ArticleCS/Print.aspx?Portal Id=1&ModuleId=682&Article=3315887.

6. Austin, "Memorandum for Senior Pentagon Leadership, Commanders of the Combatant Commands, Defense Agency, and DOD Field Activity Directors."

7. Terri Moon Cronk, "Transgender Service Members Can Now Serve Openly, Carter Announces," Defense.gov, June 30, 2016, https://www .defense.gov/News/News-Stories/Article/Article/822235/transgender-service -members-can-now-serve-openly-carter-announces.

8. Lolita C. Baldor, "Troops Who Refused COVID Vaccine Still May Face Discipline," Associated Press, February 28, 2023, https://apnews.com/article /military-covid-vaccine-discharged-congress-480088ff9348e0f9d38dd27b 05fc73e6.

9. "The Army Values," Army.mil, accessed March 3, 2023, https://www.army .mil/values.

10. Patricia Kime, "US Troops Go to Court Seeking Vaccine Exemption for Those Who've Had COVID-19," Military.com, September 29, 2021, www .military.com/daily-news/2021/09/29/us-troops-go-court-seeking-vaccine -exemption-those-whove-had-covid-19.html.

11. US District Court for the Northern District of Florida, "ORDER granting temporary restraining order," CourtListener, August 2021, https: //storage.courtlistener.com/recap/gov.uscourts.flnd.409961/gov.uscourts.flnd .409961.1.0_1.pdf.

12. Kime, "US Troops Go to Court Seeking Vaccine Exemption for Those Who've Had COVID-19."

13. Austin, "Memorandum for Mandatory Coronavirus Disease 2019 Vaccination of Department of Defense Service Members."

14. Patricia Kime and Rebecca Kheel, "16 Service Members Sue to Halt DoD's Vaccine Order," Military.com, October 19, 2021, https://www.military.com

/daily-news/2021/10/19/16-service-members-sue-halt-dods-vaccine-order
.html.

15. Bethany Blankly, "Rep. Gaetz: Navy Leader's Testimony on Military Vaccine
Mandates Contradicts IG Report," The Center Square, March 1, 2023,
https://www.thecentersquare.com/national/dod-drops-covid-19-vaccine-
mandate-for-troops/article_b1f1cabe-b885-11ed-bf66-a74c8ae8627e.html.

16. Lolita C. Baldor, "Pentagon Drops COVID-19 Vaccine Requirement for
Troops," PBS, January 10, 2023, https://www.pbs.org/newshour/politics
/pentagon-drops-covid-19-vaccine-requirement-for-troops.

17. Jim Garamond, "Service Members Must Be Vaccinated or Face
Consequences, DoD Official Says," Defense.gov, December 21, 2021, https:
//www.defense.gov/News/News-Stories/Article/Article/2881481/service
-members-must-be-vaccinated-or-face-consequences-dod-official-says.

18. Baldor, "Pentagon Drops COVID-19 Vaccine Requirement for Troops."

19. Steve Beynon, "Army Cuts Off More Than 60K Unvaccinated Guard and
Reserve Soldiers' Pay and Benefits," Military.com, July 6, 2022, www
.military.com/daily-news/2022/07/06/army-cuts-off-more-60k-unvaccinated
-guard-and-reserve-soldiers-pay-and-benefits.html.

20. Jim Garamond, "Service Members Must Be Vaccinated or Face
Consequences, DoD Official Says."

21. Lolita C. Baldor, "Military Discharging Troops for Refusing Covid Vaccine,"
AP News. February 28, 2023, https://apnews.com/article/military-covid
-vaccine-discharged-congress-480088ff9348e0f9d38dd27b05fc73e6.

22. Michael Waltz, "Letter to the Secretary of Defense regarding COVID-19
Vaccine Mandate," July 26, 2022, https://waltz.house.gov/uploadedfiles
/2022-7-26-_ng_vax_mandate.pdf.

23. Department of Defense, "Secretary of Defense Memo on Rescission of
Coronavirus Disease 2019 Vaccination Requirements for Members of the
Armed Forces," January 10, 2023, https://media.defense.gov/2023/Jan/10
/2003143118/-1/-1/1/SECRETARY-OF-DEFENSE-MEMO-ON
-RESCISSION-OF-CORONAVIRUS-DISEASE-2019-VACCINATION
-REQUIREMENTS-FOR-MEMBERS-OF-THE-ARMED-FORCES.PDF.

24. Ibid.

25. Department of Defense, "Policy Regarding Human Immunodeficiency Virus
(HIV)-Positive Personnel within the Armed Forces," June 6, 2022, https:
//media.defense.gov/2022/Jun/07/2003013398/-1/-1/1/POLICY
-REGARDING-HUMAN-IMMUNODEFICIENCY-VIRUS-POSITIVE
-PERSONNEL-WITHIN-THE-ARMED-FORCES.PDF.

26. Zachary Schermele, "Pentagon, Army Sued over Decades-Old Policy Banning Recruits with HIV," NBC News, November 11, 2022, https://www.nbcnews.com/nbc-out/out-news/pentagon-army-sued-decades-old-policy-recruits-hiv-rcna56783.

27. Caitlin M. Kenny, "Ending Covid Vax Mandate Would Divide Troops into Two Classes, Navy Secretary Says," Defense One, December 6, 2022, https://www.defenseone.com/policy/2022/12/ending-covid-vax-mandate-would-divide-troops-two-classes-navy-secretary-says/380534.

28. United States Navy, "NAVADMIN 038/23: Navy COVID-19 Vaccination Policy Update," MyNavy HR, February 2023, https://www.mynavyhr.navy.mil/Portals/55/Messages/NAVADMIN/NAV2023/NAV23038.txt?ver=B6biDbLSuj-gV-JQXM_W4w%3d%3d.

29. Department of Defense, "Secretary of Defense Memo on Rescission of Coronavirus Disease 2019 Vaccination Requirements for Members of the Armed Forces."

30. Ibid.

31. Ibid.

32. Steve Beynon, "Thousands of Troops with COVID Vaccine Exemption Requests No Longer Facing Separation as Mandate Is Gone," Military.com, January 4, 2023, https://www.military.com/daily-news/2023/01/04/thousands-of-troops-covid-vaccine-exemption-requests-no-longer-facing-separation-mandate-gone.html.

33. "Navy Updates COVID-19 Vaccination Status for Service Members," Navy.mil, May 2021, https://www.navy.mil/DesktopModules/ArticleCS/Print.aspx?PortalId=1&ModuleId=682&Article=3315887.

34. Ibid.

35. Rachel S. Cohen, "Perennial Pilot Shortage Puts Air Force in Precarious Position," *Air Force Times*, March 3, 2023, https://www.airforcetimes.com/news/your-air-force/2023/03/03/perennial-pilot-shortage-puts-air-force-in-precarious-position.

36. Michael G. Mattock, Beth J. Asch, James Hosek, and Michael Boito, *The Relative Cost-Effectiveness of Retaining versus Accessing Air Force Pilots* (Santa Monica: RAND Corporation, 2019), 12, https://www.rand.org/pubs/research_reports/RR2415.html. Also available in print form.

37. Patricia Kime, "Nearly 100 Deaths, Half a Million Cases: Toll of 3 Years of Coronavirus Pandemic on the Military," Military.com, March 28, 2023, https://www.military.com/daily-news/2023/03/28/nearly-100-deaths-half-million-cases-toll-3-years-of-coronavirus-pandemic-military.html.

38. Karin A. Orvis, *Department of Defense (DoD) Quarterly Suicide Report (QSR) 4th Quarter, CY 2021* (Washington, D.C.: Department of Defense, 2021), https://www.dspo.mil/portals/113/documents/2021QSRs/TAB%20A_20220317_OFR_rpt_Q4%20CY21%20QSR.pdf?ver=PcN7dgtBKM3RG2uP1rAZ-A%3D%3D.

Chapter 5: Diversity Doesn't Actually Make Us Stronger

1. Jim Garamond, "Biden Showcases the Strength, Excellence of American Military Diversity," Defense.gov, March 8, 2021, https://www.defense.gov/News/News-Stories/Article/Article/2529262/biden-showcases-the-strength-excellence-of-american-military-diversity.

2. Martin Luther King Jr., "I Have a Dream," speech transcript, NPR, January 16, 2023, https://www.npr.org/2010/01/18/122701268/i-have-a-dream-speech-in-its-entirety.

3. "Executive Order on Diversity, Equity, Inclusion, and Accessibility in the Federal Workforce," The White House, June 25, 2021, https://www.whitehouse.gov/briefing-room/presidential-actions/2021/06/25/executive-order-on-diversity-equity-inclusion-and-accessibility-in-the-federal-workforce.

4. "Fact Sheet: President Biden Signs Executive Order Advancing Diversity, Equity, Inclusion, and Accessibility in the Federal Government," The White House, June 25, 2021, https://www.whitehouse.gov/briefing-room/statements-releases/2021/06/25/fact-sheet-president-biden-signs-executive-order-advancing-diversity-equity-inclusion-and-accessibility-in-the-federal-government.

5. Ibid.

6. *Diversity and Inclusion Strategic Plan 2021* (SOCOM, 2021), 3, https://www.socom.mil/Documents/Diversity%20Mag%202021%20final.pdf.

7. Anna Brown, "About 5% of Young Adults in the US Say Their Gender Is Different from Their Sex Assigned at Birth," Pew Research Center, June 7, 2022, https://www.pewresearch.org/fact-tank/2022/06/07/about-5-of-young-adults-in-the-u-s-say-their-gender-is-different-from-their-sex-assigned-at-birth.

8. Rebecca Kheel, "Cotton, Pentagon Chief Tangle over Diversity Training in Military," The Hill, June 10, 2021, https://thehill.com/policy/defense/557818-cotton-pentagon-chief-tangle-over-diversity-training-in-military.

9. Rachel S. Cohen, "Air Force Leaders Set New Goals to Diversify Officer Corps," *Air Force Times*, August 30, 2022, https://www.airforcetimes.com

/news/your-air-force/2022/08/30/air-force-leaders-set-new-goals-to-diversify
-officer-corps.

10. Gina Harkins, "Air Force Will Set New Diversity Recruiting Targets for
    2021," Military.com, September 15, 2020, https://www.military.com/daily
    -news/2020/09/15/air-force-will-set-new-diversity-recruiting-targets-2021
    .html.

11. "Officer Source of Commission Applicant Pool Goals Memo," US Air Force,
    August 9, 2022, https://www.af.mil/Portals/1/documents/2022SAF
    /Officer_Source_of_Commission_Applicant_Pool_Goals_memo.pdf.

12. Thomas Novelly, "Air Force and Space Force Have New Diversity Targets
    for Their Officer Corps," Military.com, August 31, 2022, https://www
    .military.com/daily-news/2022/08/31/air-force-and-space-force-have-new
    -diversity-targets-their-officer-corps.html.

13. Rachel S. Cohen, "Here's the Air Force's Plan to Diversify Its Pilot Corps,"
    Air Force Times, March 19, 2021, https://www.airforcetimes.com/news/
    your-air-force/2021/03/19/heres-the-air-forces-plan-to-diversify-its-pilot
    -corps.

14. Chris Pandolfo, "Marine Corps Commandant Gen. David Berger: 'Zero
    Evidence' DEI Training Distracts Readiness," Fox News, March 16, 2023,
    https://www.foxnews.com/politics/marine-corps-commandant-gen-david
    -berger-zero-evidence-dei-training-distracts-readiness.

15. Mike Gallagher and Rodney Franklin, "Gallagher, Franklin Demand
    Answers from Pentagon regarding Senior Official's Racially Divisive
    Statements," House.gov, September 19, 2022, https://gallagher.house.gov
    /media/press-releases/gallagher-franklin-demand-answers-pentagon
    -regarding-senior-officials-racially.

16. Ibid.

17. Ibid.

18. Ibid.

19. Mike Brest, "Army Secretary Sees Pushback against Wokeness as Fight for
    Equality, Not Elitism," *Washington Examiner*, October 12, 2022, https:
    //www.washingtonexaminer.com/restoring-america/equality-not
    -elitism/army-secretary-wokeness-pushback-.

Chapter 6: Double Standards

1. "Women Veterans' Demographics," Department of Labor, accessed April
   22, 2023, https://www.dol.gov/agencies/vets/womenveterans/women
   veterans-demographics.

2. Cheryl Pellerin, "Carter Opens All Military Occupations, Positions to Women," Defense.gov. December 3, 2015, https://www.defense.gov/News/News-Stories/Article/Article/632536/carter-opens-all-military-occupations-positions-to-women.

3. Ibid.

4. Ibid.

5. Robert Cook, "Junior Soldier Defies All Odds to Graduate Ranger School," Army.mil, March 23, 2017, https://www.army.mil/article/184759/junior_soldier_defies_all_odds_to_graduate_ranger_school.

6. Lauren Prince and Alex Johnson, "Two Women Make History Passing Army's Elite Ranger School," NBC News, August 17, 2015, https://www.nbcnews.com/news/us-news/two-women-make-history-passing-armys-elite-ranger-school-n411506.

7. Susan Keating, "Female Rangers Were Given Special Treatment, Sources Say," People.com, September 25, 2015, https://people.com/celebrity/female-rangers-were-given-special-treatment-sources-say.

8. Ibid.

9. Ibid.

10. Ibid.

11. Dan Lamothe, "All Remaining Female Soldiers Fall Short at Ranger School's Darby Phase," *Washington Post*, May 8, 2015, https://www.washingtonpost.com/news/checkpoint/wp/2015/05/08/all-remaining-female-soldiers-fall-short-at-ranger-schools-darby-phase.

12. Keating, "Female Rangers Were Given Special Treatment, Sources Say."

13. Ibid.

14. Michelle Tan, "Congressman Wants Proof Standards Weren't Fudged for Female Ranger School Attendees," *Army Times*, September 22, 2015, https://www.armytimes.com/news/pentagon-congress/2015/09/23/congressman-wants-proof-standards-weren-t-fudged-for-female-ranger-school-attendees.

15. Susan Keating, "Some Documents Related to Females' Performance at Ranger School Shredded," *People*, October 13, 2015, https://people.com/celebrity/some-documents-related-to-females-performance-at-ranger-school-shredded.

16. Keating, "Female Rangers Were Given Special Treatment, Sources Say."

17. Philip Athey, "The Corps Can't Complete Its Missions without Women, Minorities, Top Marine Says," *Marine Corps Times*, September 11, 2020, https://www.marinecorpstimes.com/news/your-marine-corps/2020/09/11

/the-corps-cant-complete-its-missions-without-women-minorities-top
-marine-says.

18. Matthew Cox, "Army Will Require All Soldiers to Take New Combat Fitness
    Test by 2020," Military.com, July 9, 2018, https://www.military.com/daily
    -news/2018/07/09/army-will-require-all-soldiers-take-new-combat-fitness
    -test-2020.html.

19. Steve Beynon, "Nearly Half of Female Soldiers Still Failing New Army
    Fitness Test While Males Pass Easily," Military.com, May 10, 2021, https:
    //www.military.com/daily-news/2021/05/10/nearly-half-of-female-soldiers-
    still-failing-new-army-fitness-test-while-males-pass-easily.html.

20. "ACFT—Army Combat Fitness Test," accessed February 12, 2023, United
    States Army, https://www.army.mil/acft.

21. Kristin M. Geist, "With Equal Opportunity Comes Equal Responsibility:
    Lowering Fitness Standards to Accommodate Women Will Hurt the Army
    and Women," Modern War Institute at West Point, February 25, 2021,
    https://mwi.usma.edu/with-equal-opportunity-comes-equal-responsibility
    -lowering-fitness-standards-to-accommodate-women-will-hurt-the-army
    -and-women.

22. "Men 26 and Older," Selective Service System, accessed October 23, 2023,
    https://www.sss.gov/register/men-26-and-older.

23. DocumentCloud. "Selective Service Decision: National Coalition for Men
    v. Selective Service System," filed February 22, 2019. https://www
    .documentcloud.org/documents/5747780-190224-SELECTIVE-SERVICE
    -DECISION-Full.html.

24. Gregory Korte, "Federal Judge: All-Male Draft Is Unconstitutional. What
    Happens Next?" *USA Today*, February 25, 2019, https://www.usatoday
    .com/story/news/nation/2019/02/25/federal-judge-all-male-draft
    -unconstitutional-now-what-selective-service/2979346002.

25. Gregory Korte and Tom Vanden Brook, "Obama Supports Registering
    Women for Military Draft," *USA Today*, December 1, 2016, https://www
    .usatoday.com/story/news/politics/2016/12/01/obama-supports-registering
    -women-military-draft/90449708.

26. UNT Digital Library. "Final Report of the National Commission on Military,
    National and Public Service" March 2020. https://digital.library
    .unt.edu/ark:/67531/metadc1724232/m1/13.

27. "Who Needs to Register," Selective Service System, accessed October 23,
    2023, https://www.sss.gov/register/who-needs-to-register.

Chapter 7: Military Pride

1. Anna Brown, "About 5% of Young Adults in the US Say Their Gender Is Different from Their Sex Assigned at Birth," Pew Research Center, June 7, 2022, https://www.pewresearch.org/short-reads/2022/06/07/about-5-of-young-adults-in-the-u-s-say-their-gender-is-different-from-their-sex-assigned-at-birth.

2. Michael Lee, "Air Force Leaders Discourage Use of Gender-Specific Pronouns in Award Citations," Fox News, June 29, 2022, https://www.foxnews.com/us/air-force-leaders-discourage-use-gender-specific-pronouns-award-citations.

3. "Signature Block Pronouns Now Allowed for Airmen, Guardians," Airforce.mil, December 20, 2021, https://www.af.mil/News/Article-Display/Article/2879382/signature-block-pronouns-now-allowed-for-airmen-guardians.

4. Charles Pope, "Final Changes to Air Force Song Announced," Airforce.mil, May 29, 2020, https://www.af.mil/News/Article-Display/Article/2201395/final-changes-to-air-force-song-announced.

5. "The SEAL Ethos," Navy.mil, accessed on December 18, 2022, https://www.nsw.navy.mil/ABOUT-US/SEAL-Ethos.

6. John Vannucci, "NAVSpEAks—Pronouns," DVIDS, June 23, 2021, https://www.dvidshub.net/video/844401/navspeaks-pronouns.

7. Mairead Elordi, "Army Releases Woke Cartoon Recruitment Ad after Woke CIA Ads Mocked," The Daily Wire, May 13, 2021, https://www.dailywire.com/news/army-releases-woke-cartoon-recruitment-ad-after-woke-cia-ads-mocked.

8. Jon Simkins, "Sailor by Day, Performer by Night—Meet the Navy's Drag Queen, 'Harpy Daniels,'" *Military Times*, August 30, 2018, https://www.militarytimes.com/off-duty/military-culture/2018/08/30/sailor-by-day-performer-by-night-meet-the-navys-drag-queen-harpy-daniels.

9. Liz George, "Air Force Hosts Drag Show at Kid-Friendly Diversity and Inclusion Festival on Base," *American Military News*, August 1, 2022. https://americanmilitarynews.com/2022/08/air-force-hosts-drag-show-at-kid-friendly-diversity-inclusion-festival-on-base.

10. Rachel S. Cohen, "Ramstein Rethinks Pride Month Events after Critics Bash Drag Queen Story Time for Kids," *Air Force Times*, May 27, 2022, https://www.airforcetimes.com/news/your-air-force/2022/05/27/ramstein-rethinks-pride-month-events-after-critics-bash-drag-queen-story-time-for-kids.

11. Zoe Kalen Hill, "US Military Defends Drag Show at Largest Training Center as 'Essential' for Morale," *Newsweek*, June 24, 2021. https://www.newsweek.com/us-military-defends-drag-show-largest-training-center-essential-morale-1603864.

12. Michael Lee, "GOP Rep Stumps Top Military Leaders with Question on Base Drag Shows: 'First I'm Hearing That,'" Fox News. March 30, 2023, https://www.foxnews.com/politics/gop-rep-stumps-top-military-leaders-question-base-drag-shows-first-im-hearing-that.

13. Devon Suits, "Army Announces New Grooming, Appearance Standards," Army.mil, January 27, 2021, https://www.army.mil/article/242536/army_announces_new_grooming_appearance_standards.

14. Ibid.

15. Terri Moon Cronk, "Transgender Service Members Can Now Serve Openly, Carter Announces," Department of Defense, June 30, 2016, https://www.defense.gov/News/News-Stories/Article/Article/822235/transgender-service-members-can-now-serve-openly-carter-announces.

16. "The National Independent Panel on Military Service and Readiness," The Heritage Foundation, March 30, 2023, https://www.heritage.org/defense/report/report-the-national-independent-panel-military-service-and-readiness.

17. Terri Moon Cronk, "Transgender Service Members Can Now Serve Openly, Carter Announces."

18. Chrissy Clark, "Navy Guidance: Trans Men Can Use Facility That Corresponds To Their Gender Identity; Misgendering Leads To Unlawful Hostile Work Environment," The Daily Wire, July 9. 2021, https://www.dailywire.com/news/navy-guidance-trans-men-can-use-facility-that-corresponds-to-their-gender-identity-misgendering-leads-to-unlawful-hostile-work-environment.

19. "The National Independent Panel on Military Service and Readiness," The Heritage Foundation, March 30, 2023, https://www.heritage.org/defense/report/report-the-national-independent-panel-military-service-and-readiness.

20. Patricia Kime, "Here's How Much the Pentagon Has Spent So Far to Treat Transgender Troops," Military.com, June 18, 2021, https://www.military.com/daily-news/2021/06/18/heres-how-much-pentagon-has-spent-so-far-treat-transgender-troops.html.

21. Terri Moon Cronk, "DOD Revises Transgender Policies to Align with White House," Defense.gov, March 31, 2021, https://www.defense.gov/News

/News-Stories/Article/Article/2557118/dod-revises-transgender-policies-to -align-with-white-house.

22. "What Is Gender Dysphoria?," American Psychiatric Association, accessed on February 26, 2023, https://www.psychiatry.org/patients-families/gender -dysphoria/what-is-gender-dysphoria.

23. Terri Moon Cronk, "Transgender Service Members Can Now Serve Openly, Carter Announces."

24. Thomas Novelly, "New Pentagon Study Shows 77% of Young Americans are Ineligible for Military Service," Military.com, September 28, 2022, https://www.military.com/daily-news/2022/09/28/new-pentagon-study -shows-77-of-young-americans-are-ineligible-military-service.html.

25. "Disqualifications," United States Air Force Academy, accessed April 19, 2023. https://www.academyadmissions.com/requirements/medical /disqualifications.

26. *Woke Warfighters: A Report on the Department of Defense's Cultural Revolution* (Washington, D.C.: Rubio Senate, 2021), 10, https://www.rubio .senate.gov/public/_cache/files/ee1d7a86-6d0c-4f08-bd15-24e5b28e54b7 /3756824FA9C21B819BB97AAB16221530.woke-warfighters-report-3.pdf.

27. Adam Edelman, "Trump Announces Ban on Transgender People Serving in Military," NBC News, July 26, 2017, https://www.nbcnews.com/politics /donald-trump/trump-announces-ban-transgender-people-serving-military -n786621.

28. "5 Things to Know about DOD's New Policy on Military Service by Transgender Persons and Persons with Gender Dysphoria," Department of Defense, March 13, 2019, https://www.defense.gov/News/News-Stories /Article/Article/1783822/5-things-to-know-about-dods-new-policy-on -military-service-by-transgender-perso.

29. Ibid.

30. "Fact Sheet: Biden-Harris Administration Advances Equality and Visibility for Transgender Americans," The White House, March 31, 2022, https: //www.whitehouse.gov/briefing-room/statements-releases/2022/03/31/fact- sheet-biden-harris-administration-advances-equality-and-visibility-for -transgender-americans.

31. Christie Smetana, "Cosmetic Surgery in the Military Has Considerations, Limitations," Joint Base Charleston, September 5, 2018, https://www .jbcharleston.jb.mil/News/Commentaries/Display/Article/1619396/cosmetic -surgery-in-the-military-has-considerations-limitations.

32. "Department of Defense Instruction: In-Service Transition for Transgender Service Members," Department of Defense, December 20, 2022, https://www.esd.whs.mil/Portals/54/Documents/DD/issuances/dodi/130028p.pdf.

33. Susan B. Glasser and Peter Baker, "Inside the War between Trump and His Generals," *New Yorker*, August 15, 2022, https://www.newyorker.com/magazine/2022/08/15/inside-the-war-between-trump-and-his-generals.

34. *Woke Warfighters: A Report on the Department of Defense's Cultural Revolution*, 11.

35. Rebecca Kheel, "Pentagon Quietly Looking at How Nonbinary Troops Could Serve Openly," Military.com, January 18, 2022, https://www.military.com/daily-news/2022/01/18/pentagon-quietly-looking-how-nonbinary-troops-could-serve-openly.html.

Chapter 8: Another Forgotten War

1. "NATO and Afghanistan," NATO, May 30, 2022, https://www.nato.int/cps/en/natolive/topics_69366.htm.

2. *What We Need to Learn: Lessons of Twenty Years of Afghanistan Reconstruction* (Arlington, Virginia: SIGAR, 2021), https://www.sigar.mil/pdf/lessonslearned/SIGAR-21-46-LL.pdf.

3. Kristi Keck, "Obama: Troop Increase Needed in Afghanistan," CNN, September 28, 2009, https://www.cnn.com/2009/POLITICS/09/28/afghanistan.obama/index.html.

4. *Quarterly Report to the United States Congress* (Arlington, Virginia: SIGAR, 2017), https://www.sigar.mil/pdf/quarterlyreports/2017-10-30qr.pdf.

5. David H. Petraeus, "The Situation in Afghanistan," US Department of Defense, March 15, 2011, https://ogc.osd.mil/Portals/99/testPetraeus0315 2011.pdf.

6. Craig Whitlock, "Afghan Security Forces' Wholesale Collapse Was Years in the Making," *Washington Post*, August 16, 2021, https://www.washingtonpost.com/investigations/afghan-security-forces-capabilities/2021/08/15/052a45e2-fdc7-11eb-a664-4f6de3e17ff0_story.html.

7. Ibid.

8. Ibid.

9. John F. Campbell, "Operation Freedom's Sentinel and Our Continued Security Investment in Afghanistan," Army.mil, October 5, 2015, https://www.army.mil/article/156517/operation_freedoms_sentinel_and_our_continued_security_investment_in_afghanistan.

10. "Trump Pledges to Withdraw Troops from Afghanistan by Christmas as Taliban Cheer," NBC News, October 8, 2020, https://www.nbcnews.com/news/world/trump-pledges-withdraw-troops-afghanistan-christmas-taliban-cheer-n1242590.

11. Robert Burns and Lolita C. Baldor, "Pentagon Says US Has Dropped to 2500 Troops in Afghanistan," Associated Press, January 15, 2021, https://apnews.com/article/donald-trump-afghanistan-joe-biden-united-states-coronavirus-pandemic-c76ed7d4c96c4f7cb524f1b3924f2956.

12. Jim Garamone, "Afghan Forces Have Capacity to Fight, Defend Country, Milley Says," Department of Defense, July 21, 2021, https://www.defense.gov/News/News-Stories/Article/Article/2702101/afghan-forces-have-capacity-to-fight-defend-country-milley-says.

13. Joe Biden, "Remarks by President Biden on the Drawdown of US Forces in Afghanistan," White House, July 8, 2021, https://www.whitehouse.gov/briefing-room/speeches-remarks/2021/07/08/remarks-by-president-biden-on-the-drawdown-of-u-s-forces-in-afghanistan.

14. Ibid.

15. "Human and Budgetary Costs to Date of the US War in Afghanistan, 2001–2022," Brown University, August 2021, https://watson.brown.edu/costsofwar/figures/2021/human-and-budgetary-costs-date-us-war-afghanistan-2001-2022.

16. Lara Seligman, "Speed Equals Safety: How the Pentagon's Controversial Decision to Leave Bagram Early," Politico, September 28, 2021, https://www.politico.com/news/2021/09/28/pentagon-decision-leave-bagram-514456.

17. "Why the Afghanistan Withdrawal Was the Perfect Storm of Bureaucratic Incompetence," townhall.com, August 15, 2022. https://townhall.com/columnists/ambersmith/2022/08/15/why-the-afghanistan-withdrawal-was-the-perfect-storm-of-bureaucratic-incompetence-n2611606.

18. Ibid.

19. John Grady, "CENTCOM: Keeping Bagram Airbase Was Untenable under White House Rules for Afghanistan Withdrawal," USNI News, September 29, 2021, https://news.usni.org/2021/09/29/centcom-keeping-bagram-airbase-was-untenable-under-white-house-rules-for-afghanistan-withdrawal.

20. "Why the Afghanistan Withdrawal Was the Perfect Storm of Bureaucratic Incompetence," townhall.com, August 15, 2022. https://townhall.com/columnists/ambersmith/2022/08/15/why-the-afghanistan-withdrawal-was-the-perfect-storm-of-bureaucratic-incompetence-n2611606.

21. Ibid.

22. Ivana Saric, "Thousands of Prisoners Freed by Taliban Could Pose Threat to US," Axios, August 15, 2021, https://www.axios.com/2021/08/15/taliban-bagram-prisoners-release.

23. Junaid Kathju, "US Arms Left in Afghanistan Are Turning Up in a Different Conflict," NBC News, January 30, 2023. https://www.nbcnews.com/news/world/us-weapons-afghanistan-taliban-kashmir-rcna67134.

24. "New Evidence: Biometric Data Systems Imperil Afghans," Human Rights Watch, March 30, 2022, https://www.hrw.org/news/2022/03/30/new-evidence-biometric-data-systems-imperil-afghans.

25. Robert Burns and Josh Boak, "Biden Orders 1,000 More Troops to Aid Afghanistan Departure," AP News, August 14, 2021, https://apnews.com/article/lifestyle-joe-biden-middle-east-evacuations-kabul-8ec855b3f943dafe80d3d3ca6b0953f2.

26. Dan Lamothe and Alex Horton, "Documents Reveal US Military's Frustration with White House, Diplomats over Afghanistan Evacuation," *Washington Post*, February 8, 2022, https://www.washingtonpost.com/national-security/2022/02/08/afghanistan-evacuation-investigation.

27. Burns and Boak, "Biden Orders 1,000 More Troops to Aid Afghanistan Departure."

28. "Why the Afghanistan Withdrawal Was the Perfect Storm of Bureaucratic Incompetence," townhall.com, August 15, 2022. https://townhall.com/columnists/ambersmith/2022/08/15/why-the-afghanistan-withdrawal-was-the-perfect-storm-of-bureaucratic-incompetence-n2611606.

29. Michael D. Shear, David E. Sanger, Helene Cooper, Eric Schmitt, Julian E. Barnes, and Lara Jakes, "Miscue after Miscue, US Exit Plan Unravels," *New York Times*, August 31, 2021, https://www.nytimes.com/2021/08/21/us/politics/biden-taliban-afghanistan-kabul.html.

30. "Why the Afghanistan Withdrawal Was the Perfect Storm of Bureaucratic Incompetence," townhall.com, August 15, 2022. https://townhall.com/columnists/ambersmith/2022/08/15/why-the-afghanistan-withdrawal-was-the-perfect-storm-of-bureaucratic-incompetence-n2611606.

31. Costs of War Project, "Human and Budgetary Costs to Date of the US War in Afghanistan, 2001–2022."

32. "Why the Afghanistan Withdrawal Was the Perfect Storm of Bureaucratic Incompetence," townhall.com, August 15, 2022. https://townhall.com/columnists/ambersmith/2022/08/15/why-the-afghanistan-withdrawal-was-the-perfect-storm-of-bureaucratic-incompetence-n2611606.

33. House.gov, "National Security Officials Confirm Rep. Calvert: Kabul Bomber Was Previously Held at Guantanamo Bay," press release, September 28, 2021. https://calvert.house.gov/media/press-releases/national-security -officials-confirm-rep-calvert-kabul-bomber-was-previously.

34. Yaroslav Trofimov and Vivian Salama, "In Its Last Days in Kabul, US Turns to Taliban as a Partner," *Wall Street Journal*, August 27, 2021, www .wsj.com/articles/in-its-last-days-in-kabul-u-s-turns-to-taliban-as-a-partner -11630105650.

35. Sandi Sidhu, Nick Paton Walsh, Tim Lister, Oren Liebermann, Laura Smith-Spark, and Saskya Vandoorne. "Ten Family Members, Including Children, Dead after US Strike in Kabul," CNN, August 30, 2021, https: //www.cnn.com/2021/08/29/asia/afghanistan-kabul-evacuation-intl/index .html.

36. Anna Coren, Julia Hollingsworth, Sandi Sidhu, and Zachary Cohen, "US Military Admits It Killed 10 Civilians and Targeted Wrong Vehicle in Kabul Airstrike," CNN, September 17, 2021, https://www.cnn.com/2021/09/17 /politics/kabul-drone-strike-us-military-intl-hnk/index.html.

37. Matthieu Aikins, "Times Investigation: In US Drone Strike, Evidence Suggests No ISIS Bomb," *New York Times*, January 5, 2022, https://www .nytimes.com/2021/09/10/world/asia/us-air-strike-drone-kabul-afghanistan -isis.html.

38. Sophie Reardon, "US Military Admits Kabul Drone Strike Was 'a Mistake,' Killing Civilians," CBS News, September 17, 2021, https://www .cbsnews.com/news/afghanistan-drone-strike-mistake-civilians-killed -pentagon.

39. Anna Coren, Julia Hollingsworth, Sandi Sidhu, and Zachary Cohen, "US military admits it killed 10 civilians and targeted wrong vehicle in Kabul airstrike."

40. "Marine Corps Sergeant Tyler Vargas-Andrews testifies in front of congress on Abby Gate," YouTube video, March 9, 2023, 9:44, https://www .youtube.com/watch?v=qNs8QSGcCcg.

41. Ibid.

42. Ibid.

43. Ibid.

44. *ADP 6-0: Mission Command* (Washington, D.C.: Department of the Army, 2019), 15, https://armypubs.army.mil/epubs/DR_pubs/DR_a/ARN34403-ADP_6-0-000-WEB-3.pdf.

45. Michael Lee, "Marine Sniper Tears Up Testifying How Leaders Ignored His Warnings Minutes before Kabul Airport Blast," Fox News, March 8, 2023, https://www.foxnews.com/world/marine-sniper-tears-up-testifying -how-leaders-ignored-his-warnings-minutes-before-kabul-airport-blast.

46. Ibid.

47. Elisha Fieldstadt, "The Last Soldier to Leave Afghanistan—Nicknamed 'Flatliner'—Was Uniquely Prepared for That Moment," NBC News, September 1, 2021, https://www.nbcnews.com/news/world/last-soldier-leave -afghanistan-nicknamed-flatliner-was-uniquely-prepared-moment -n1278260.

48. Craig Whitlock, "A War With The Truth," *Washington Post*, December 9, 2019, https://www.washingtonpost.com/graphics/2019/investigations /afghanistan-papers/afghanistan-war-confidential-documents.

49. Ibid.

50. "Afghanistan Paper: A Secret History of the War," *Washington Post*, December 9, 2019, https://www.washingtonpost.com/graphics/2019 /investigations/afghanistan-papers/documents-database/?document =background_ll_07_xx_woodbridge_08032016.

51. Scott Wong and Haley Talbot, "Veterans Deliver Emotional, Scathing Testimony about 'Disastrous' Afghanistan Withdrawal," Yahoo News, March 8, 2023, https://news.yahoo.com/house-gop-kicks-off-first -130000197.html.

52. "McCaul Delivers Opening Remarks at Full Committee Hearing Examining Admin's Disastrous Evacuation from Afghanistan," US House of Representatives Committee on Foreign Affairs, March 8, 2023. https: //foreignaffairs.house.gov/press-release/mccaul-delivers-opening-remarks-at -full-committee-hearing-examining-admins-disastrous-evacuation-from -afghanistan.

53. Ibid.

54. Deirdre Walsh, "An Injured Marine Gives Searing Testimony on the Chaotic Withdrawal from Afghanistan," WBUR, March 8, 2023, https: //www.wbur.org/npr/1161890168/house-republicans-hearing-withdrawal -afghanistan-biden.

55. Wong and Talbot, "Veterans Deliver Emotional, Scathing Testimony about 'Disastrous' Afghanistan Withdrawal."

Chapter 9: Rewriting History

1. Russell Vought, *Memorandum for the Heads of Executive Departments and Agencies* (Washington, D.C.: Executive Office of the President, 2020), 1, https://www.whitehouse.gov/wp-content/uploads/2020/09/M-20-34.pdf.

2. Donald J. Trump (@realDonaldTrump), "A few weeks ago, I BANNED efforts to indoctrinate government employees with divisive and harmful sex and race-based ideologies. Today, I've expanded that ban to people and companies that do business. . ." Twitter, September 22, 2020, 5:53 p.m., https://twitter.com/realDonaldTrump/status/1308539918075883523.

3. "Government-Wide Diversity and Inclusion Strategic Plan 2011," Office of Personnel Management, accessed April 3, 2023, https://www.opm.gov/policy-data-oversight/diversity-equity-inclusion-and-accessibility/reports/governmentwidedistrategicplan.pdf.

4. Vought, *Memorandum for the Heads of Executive Departments and Agencies*.

5. Executive Order on Combating Race and Sex Stereotyping, September 22, 2020, Trump White House Archives, accessed January 14, 2023, https://trumpwhitehouse.archives.gov/presidential-actions/executive-order-combating-race-sex-stereotyping.

6. "Fact Sheet: President-elect Biden's Day One Executive Actions Deliver Relief for Families Across America Amid Converging Crises," White House, January 20, 2021, https://www.whitehouse.gov/briefing-room/statements-releases/2021/01/20/fact-sheet-president-elect-bidens-day-one-executive-actions-deliver-relief-for-families-across-america-amid-converging-crises.

7. "Advancing Racial Equity and Support for Underserved Communities Through the Federal Government," Executive Office of the President, Federal Register, January 25, 2021, https://www.federalregister.gov/documents/2021/01/25/2021-01753/advancing-racial-equity-and-support-for-underserved-communities-through-the-federal-government.

8. "Advancing Racial Equity and Support for Underserved Communities Through the Federal Government."

9. Wicker Senate, "Military Has Spent 6 Million Man-Hours on 'Woke' Training under Biden, Senators Find," press release, February 15, 2022, https://www.wicker.senate.gov/2022/2/military-has-spent-6-million-man-hours-on-woke-training-under-biden-senators-find.

10. Bryan Anderson, "So Much Buzz, but What Is Critical Race Theory?" AP News, June 24, 2021, https://apnews.com/article/what-is-critical-race-theory-08f5d0a0489c7d6eab7d9a238365d2c1.

11. Jacey Fortin, "Critical Race Theory: A Brief History," *New York Times*, November 8, 2021, https://www.nytimes.com/article/what-is-critical-race-theory.html.

12. Mike Brest, "Air Force Academy Requires Training Linked to Critical Race Theory and Black Lives Matter," *Washington Examiner*, August 18, 2021, https://www.washingtonexaminer.com/news/air-force-academy-requires-training-linked-critical-race-theory-black-lives-matter.

13. Audrey Conklin, "Navy Won't Remove 'Anti-American' Books from Reading List despite House Republicans' Concerns," Fox News, March 16, 2021, https://www.foxnews.com/politics/navy-reading-list-republican-concerns.

14. Ibram X. Kendi (@drIbram), "I keep saying there's no such thing as being 'not racist.' We are either being racist or antiracist. And in order to be antiracist, we must, first and foremost, be willing to admit the times we are being racist, which #AmyCooper failed to do, which many Amy Coopers fail to do," Twitter, May 26, 2020, 10:13 a.m., https://twitter.com/DrIbram/status/1265300114849087488.

15. Paul Szoldra, "Why the US Navy Wants Sailors to Read 'How To Be an Antiracist,'" Task & Purpose, June 23, 2021, https://taskandpurpose.com/news/us-navy-reading-list-how-to-be-an-antiracist.

16. Louis Casiano and Lucas Y. Tomlinson, "US Military First Shot at Unknown Octagonal Object in Lake Huron Missed, Officials Say," Fox News, February 13, 2023. https://www.foxnews.com/us/us-military-first-shot-unknown-octagonal-object-lake-huron-missed.

17. "Watch: Seek to Understand, Microaggressions," United States Air Force Academy, August 17, 2020, https://www.usafa.af.mil/News/Article/2314621/watch-seek-to-understand-microaggressions.

18. Lynne Chandler García, "I'm a Professor at a US Military Academy. Here's Why I Teach Critical Race Theory," *Washington Post*, July 6, 2021, https://www.washingtonpost.com/opinions/2021/07/06/military-academies-should-teach-critical-race-theory.

19. Michael Lee, "Air Force Academy Requires Students to Watch 'Inclusion' Training Video Promoting BLM," Fox News, August 19, 2021, https://www.foxnews.com/politics/air-force-academy-requires-students-students-to-watch-inclusion-training-video-promoting-blm.

20. Jessica Chasmar, "Air Force Academy Diversity Training Tells Cadets to Use Words That 'Include All Genders,' Drop 'Mom and Dad,'" Fox News, September 22, 2022, https://www.foxnews.com/politics/air-force-academy

-diversity-training-tells-cadets-to-use-words-that-include-all-genders-drop-mom-and-dad.

21. Ibid.

22. Secretary of the Air Force Public Affairs, "Diversity and Inclusion update." United States Air Force Academy, July 27, 2020, https://www.usafa.af.mil/News/Article/2278332/diversity-and-inclusion-update.

23. Ibid.

24. US Air Force Recruiting, "US Air Force: Unconscious Bias," YouTube video, 3:14, October 7, 2020. https://www.youtube.com/watch?v=y8OL1_Q6vzg.

25. "Application to become a Brooke Owens Fellow in the Class of 2023," Brooke Owens Fellowship, accessed on March 24, 2023, https://static1.squarespace.com/static/577f2528bebafb28867da673/t/6310ba86e06c9131de7cf402/1662040710715/BOF_ClassOf23_Application.pdf.

26. Ibid.

27. Chrissy Clark, "Exclusive: Navy Established Group To Develop 'Inclusive' Artwork For Naval Offices," The Daily Wire, June 2, 2021, https://www.dailywire.com/news/exclusive-navy-established-group-to-develop-inclusive-artwork-for-naval-offices.

28. C-SPAN, "Secretary of Defense & Joint Chiefs Chair Respond to Rep. Matt Gaetz on Critical Race Theory," YouTube video, 3:06, June 23, 2021, https://www.youtube.com/watch?v=3uIZ4C3Y0Ng&t=93s.

29. García, "I'm a Professor at a US Military Academy. Here's Why I Teach Critical Race Theory."

30. C-SPAN, "Secretary of Defense & Joint Chiefs Chair Respond to Rep. Matt Gaetz on Critical Race Theory."

31. Ibid.

32. Tom Bowman and Steve Walsh, "The Military Confronts Extremism, One Conversation at a Time," NPR, April 7, 2021, https://www.npr.org/2021/04/07/984700148/the-military-confronts-extremism-one-conversation-at-a-time.

33. C-SPAN, "Secretary of Defense & Joint Chiefs Chair Respond to Rep. Matt Gaetz on Critical Race Theory."

34. House.gov, "Waltz Requests Critical Race Theory Materials & Presentations from West Point," press release, April 8, 2021, https://waltz.house.gov/news/documentsingle.aspx?DocumentID=486.

35. Ibid.

Chapter 10: The All-Volunteer Force Is Failing

1. *2021 Demographics: Profile of the Military Community* (Washington, D.C.: Department of Defense, 2021), 40, https://download.militaryonesource .mil/12038/MOS/Reports/2021-demographics-report.pdf.

2. David Vergun, "First Peacetime Draft Enacted Just before World War II," Department of Defense, April 7, 2020, https://www.defense.gov/News /Feature-Stories/story/Article/2140942/first-peacetime-draft-enacted-just -before-world-war-ii.

3. "Historical Timeline." Selective Service System, accessed March 24, 2023, https://www.sss.gov/history-and-records/timeline.

4. Ibid.

5. Ibid.

6. Ibid.

7. Vergun, "First Peacetime Draft Enacted Just before World War II."

8. "Historical Timeline."

9. Ibid.

10. Ibid.

11. Katherine Schaeffer, "The Changing Face of America's Veteran Population," Pew Research Center, April 5, 2021, https://www.pewresearch.org/short -reads/2021/04/05/the-changing-face-of-americas-veteran-population.

12. "Historical Timeline."

13. "50 USC 3811: Offenses and penalties," Ch 49, Military Selective Service, accessed February 22, 2023, http://uscode.house.gov/view.xhtml?hl=false& edition=prelim&path=%2Fprelim%40title50%2Fchapter49&req=granul eid%3AUSC-prelim-title50-section3811.

14. Jim Absher, "Everything You Need to Know about the Military Draft," Military.com, March 1, 2023, https://www.military.com/join-armed-forces /everything-you-need-know-about-military-selective-service-system.html.

15. Gregory Korte, "For a Million US Men, Failing to Register for the Draft Has Serious, Long-Term Consequences," *USA Today*, April 2, 2019, https: //www.usatoday.com/story/news/nation/2019/04/02/failing-register-draft -women-court-consequences-men/3205425002.

16. Inspired to Serve: National Commission on Military, National, and Public Service, 2020, page 11, accessed January 23, 2023, https://digital.library.unt .edu/ark:/67531/metadc1724232/m1/13.

17. Aaron Zitner, "America Pulls Back From Values That Once Defined It, WSJ-NORC Poll Finds," *Wall Street Journal*, March 27, 2023, https://www

.wsj.com/articles/americans-pull-back-from-values-that-once-defined-u-s-wsj
-norc-poll-finds-df8534cd.

18. Schaeffer, "The Changing Face of America's Veteran Population."

19. Joe Davidson, "Military Recruiting Lapses Lead to 'Challenges to National
Security,'" *Washington Post*, April 21, 2023, https://www.washingtonpost
.com/politics/2023/04/21/military-recruitment-lapses-national
-security-gao.

20. Office of People Analytics, *Fall 2021 Propensity Update* (Washington, D.C.:
US Department of Defense, 2022), 15, https://jamrs.defense.gov
/Portals/20/Documents/YP51Fall2021PUBLICRELEASEPropensityUpdate
.pdf.

21. "Veterans with Amputations & Limb Loss," Disabled American Veterans,
accessed March 22, 2023, https://www.dav.org/get-help-now/veteran-topics
-resources/veterans-with-amputations-limb-loss.

22. "Facts and Figures," Army.mil, accessed February 6, 2023, https:
//recruiting.army.mil/pao/facts_figures.

23. Jeffrey M. Jones, "Confidence in US Institutions Down; Average at New
Low," Gallup News, July 5, 2022, https://news.gallup.com/poll/394283
/confidence-institutions-down-average-new-low.aspx.

24. Gregory C. McCarthy, "Are There Too Many General Officers for Today's
Military?" National Defense University Press, October 1, 2017, https:
//ndupress.ndu.edu/Publications/Article/1325984/are-there-too-many
-general-officers-for-todays-military.

Chapter 11: The Alarm

1. "National Defense Strategy," Department of Defense, 2018, accessed
February 4, 2023, https://dod.defense.gov/Portals/1/Documents/pubs/2018
-National-Defense-Strategy-Summary.pdf.

2. "Read for Yourself: The Full Memo from AMC Gen. Mike Minihan," *Air
& Space Forces Magazine*, January 30, 2023. https://www.airandspaceforces
.com/read-full-memo-from-amc-gen-mike-minihan.

3. Ibid.

4. Chris Gordon, "Pentagon Distances Itself from Minihan Memo Suggesting
Possible War with China in 2025," *Air & Space Forces Magazine*, January
29, 2023, https://www.airandspaceforces.com/pentagon-distances-itself
-minihan-memo-possible-war-china-2025.

5. Antony J. Blinken, Lloyd J. Austin III, Hayashi Yoshimasa, and Hamada
Yasukazu, "Secretary of State Antony J. Blinken, Secretary of Defense Lloyd

J. Austin III, Japanese Foreign Minister Hayashi Yoshimasa and Japanese Defense Minister Hamada Yasukazu at a Joint Press Availability," Transcript, Department of Defense, January 11, 2023, https://www.defense.gov/News /Transcripts/Transcript/Article/3265802/secretary-of-state-antony-j-blinken -secretary-of-defense-lloyd-j-austin-iii-jap.

6. "Air Force Small Business," Air Mobility Command, accessed April 2, 2023, https://www.airforcesmallbiz.af.mil/AMC/#:~:text=Air%20Mobility %20Command%27s%20mission%20is,all%20of%20America%27s %20armed%20forces.

7. Mike Gilday, "How Will the US Navy Navigate an Uncertain Security Environment? A Conversation with ADM Mike Gilday," Atlantic Council, Video, 54:42, May 4, 2021, https://www.youtube.com/watch?v =7UfKN4oU22g&t=2s.

8. Mallory Shelbourne, "Davidson: China Could Try to Take Control of Taiwan in 'Next Six Years,'" USNI News, March 9, 2021, https://news.usni .org/2021/03/09/davidson-china-could-try-to-take-control-of-taiwan-in-next -six-years.

9. Jerry Hendrix, "Closing the Davidson Window," RealClearDefense, July 3, 2021, https://www.realcleardefense.com/articles/2021/07/03/closing_the _davidson_window_784100.html.

10. Geoff Ziezulewicz, "Pentagon: Yes, We Are Still Lagging behind China's Hypersonics," *Navy Times*, April 18, 2023, https://www.navytimes.com /news/your-navy/2023/04/18/pentagon-yes-we-are-still-lagging-behind -chinas-hypersonics.

11. Ibid.

12. Stephen Losey, "ARRW Hypersonic Missile Test Failed, US Air Force Admits," *Defense News*, March 28, 2023, https://www.defensenews.com /air/2023/03/28/arrw-hypersonic-missile-test-failed-us-air-force-admits.

13. Ziezulewicz, "Pentagon: Yes, We Are Still Lagging behind China's Hypersonics."

14. "How Thomas Paine's Other Pamphlet Saved the Revolution," Constitution Center, December 19, 2022, https://constitutioncenter.org/blog/ how-thomas-paines-other-pamphlet-saved-the-revolution.

ACKNOWLEDGMENTS

I was inspired to write this book after the Pentagon's response to the recruitment crisis in 2022. Most of the military branches didn't meet their numbers, and all we heard was excuse after excuse from the service secretaries, chief of staff, generals, pentagon officials, etc. They talked about everything except the reality of the situation. They just couldn't seem to articulate the reason behind young Americans no longer wanting to join the military. And since they refused to acknowledge the problem, I decided I would. Those who care about the military will want to fix it. I am incredibly grateful to have been given the opportunity to write this book and shed light on this urgent and dire issue, and for all who helped along the way.

Most importantly, I want to thank my wonderful and amazing husband, Andy. This book could not have been written without you. Your constant support and motivation, your willingness to change your insanely busy schedule, travel, and meetings to ensure I had time for all of my research, interviews, and writing made this all possible. You have always been my biggest supporter, and I am so grateful for that. Your encouragement through this entire project has made all the difference. And a very special thank you to my children, who saw their mom a little less than usual while I was doing my heavy research and writing. Thank you all for your love and patience and for giving purpose to everything. I am the luckiest person in the world to have you all.

Thank you to my parents, Lane and Betsy, for introducing me to the incredible world of aviation and instilling in me a patriotic love of country from when I was a young child. Thank you for teaching me the importance of critical and independent thinking and the value of freedom. And for all of your help along the way.

I owe a great deal to all of the Active Duty, Guard, Reserve service members, and recent veterans who spoke with me throughout my research for this book, most of whom I will not name. Many were rightfully extremely concerned about retaliation (including those out of the military) but spoke to me anyway. I appreciate your trust and taking the time to share the truth. You all made great sacrifices for our nation, and I thank you: Grant Smith, Ian Patterson, David Hamski, Matt Fogg, Nic Adams, and the many others who will remain anonymous.

A very big thank you to my long-time friend Joey Jones for the conversation years ago, which helped light the spark for this book. Thank you for your service to our country and for always using your valuable voice to speak the truth. Thank you for everything and your continual support!

To David Hamski. Thank you for bravely telling your story. Thank you for standing up to a machine that abused their authority. I know the strength that took, and I am in awe. You had the book thrown at you and had everything, including your very bright and promising career, taken away from you. You were proven right.

To Ian Patterson. Thank you for telling your story. It was an honor to serve with you at Jbad in Afghanistan. Air CAV!

I want to thank the service members who continue to serve and protect our nation despite the severe challenges of dealing with double standards and a two-tiered justice system, as well as facing some of the horrible policies forced upon them by the Pentagon. I am incredibly grateful for all you do. You and your families deserve better than what you are currently getting right now. Thank you for keeping watch.

To my incredible agent, Scott Kaufman, at Buchwald. I am honored to call you a friend. I am so grateful for your support and to have worked with you over the years. You are a true pro, and I am thankful to have you on my side. Thank you.

To my Regnery editor, Tony Daniel, for seeing the vision of my book from the get-go and being a fantastic editor. It has been a pleasure working with you and the entire Regnery team. Thank you for working your magic and for all your help along the way.

To Michael Baker, my assistant editor. I learned so much from you. You're an expert at what you do, and I am so grateful to you for your wisdom, opinion, and guidance. Thank you for your patience and expertise. I am still in awe of your organizational skills!

To my Skyhorse editor, Elizabeth Kantor, thank you for your grace and help throughout this process!

Special thanks to one of my best friends, Katie Pavlich. You have been so incredibly supportive, loyal, encouraging, and inspiring since day one. Thank you for everything. I am so grateful for you! And thank you for being such an amazing friend and advocate of the military and veteran community and always standing for the truth!

To General Keith Kellogg. Your service to our country, both in uniform and later in the Trump administration, is an inspiration. I am incredibly grateful for your kindness, generosity, and support throughout the years. Thank you!

To my long-time friend, Buck Sexton, who gave me my first-ever TV appearance a very long time ago. Thank you for believing in me back then and for your continued support over the years. Thank you, and get the bulldog!

Big thanks to my friend, Jesse Kelly, the host of the *Jesse Kelly* Show! You are a legend and brilliant at what you do. Thank you again.

To my friend, Lisa Boothe, who is the host of the awesome podcast The Truth with Lisa Boothe. Thank you so much for your support with *Unfit to Fight!*

To my friend, Margaux, who lived through all of the craziness that comes with writing a book with me. Your support and kindness is remarkable, and we are so grateful to have you in our lives. Thank you for everything!

To Don Bentley, *New York Times* bestselling author and former Apache pilot, thank you for your continued support! It is greatly appreciated!

To all of the incredible people who have continued to support me over the years with *Danger Close*, TV, columns, social media, newsletters, everything, you all make this possible. I promise it does not go unnoticed, and I am grateful for every one of you.

INDEX